AF431631

Resilient Dreamer

A MEMOIR

MARYSIA TARNOPOLSKA WEISS

Copyright © 2024 by Marysia Tarnopolska Weiss

Book Design and Interior by Kat Hargrave

All rights reserved. This book or any portion thereof may not be reproduced or used in any manner whatsoever without the express written permission of the publisher except for the use of brief quotations in a book review.

Printed in the United States of America

First Printing, 2024

Hardcover 979-8-9908764-0-8

Paperback 979-8-9908764-1-5

eBook 979-8-9908764-2-2

ADVANCE PRAISE FOR
Resilient Dreamer

"Growing up under a communist regime, then navigating the challenges of immigration, Marysia's story is a testament to the hope and strength of the human spirit. She shares powerful insights and inspiring stories of the power of education and perseverance in forging a path forward ultimately breaking barriers for females in STEM."

—Olga Custodio, first female Hispanic U.S. military pilot, former United States Air Force officer

"Enlightening and empowering read! Marysia goes the extra mile in sharing research on her Polish ancestors while bringing her story to present-day America. She delivers the playful side of an astute mathematics professor and mentor to thousands, striking just the right tone and pace of a no-frills memoir, coupled with riveting stories of women like her mother, who rescued Jews during the Holocaust. Resilience runs in the family. For many, so does the American dream."

—Marcia-Elizabeth C. Favale, Tech Entrepreneur and Inventor, and Author of *Leading Innovation and Inclusion and Risk, Recovery, and Empowerment: The Kazakhstan Bank Recovery Case Study*

"Marysia Tarnopolska Weiss, the resilient dreamer, shares her dream starting when it formed in the generations before her. In rich detail, she keeps her memories alive, defying the relentless march of time and the brutality of history. In her story, Marysia unlocks that of her parents and grandparents while showing us a country in a crisis of identity but never a crisis of strength. What she became in America is an exceptional thinker, teacher, and critic of culture. Great read!"

—Yuda Friedman, Author of *Reborn at the Library: From Me'a She'arim to Bogota*

"Marysia Tarnopolska Weiss's *Resilient Dreamer* brings the reader along a heartfelt, perilous and hopeful journey across cultures and continents to the dream of a new life and an everlasting home, a dream sought by so many."

—Greg Morley, Cultural Competency Thought Leader and Advisor, and Author of *Bond: Belonging and the Keys to Inclusion and Connection*

"In reading Marysia's journey, we are all reminded that we are not born resilient. As with any attribute that propels us into our future, we are taught at a very young age how to survive and thrive. While the journey oftentimes is difficult and unimaginable, the foundation that was laid by her parents and loved ones provided the strength needed to persevere into her own greatness. May we all remember

and embrace our foundations and live into becoming a
Resilient Dreamer."

—Donna M. Wilson, President of Strategic Intersections LLC,
   and Author of *Behind the Glass Doors: The Unwritten Rules
   for Success and Fulfillment*

"*Resilient Dreamer* is a beautifully written and powerful
memoir that offers a unique, deeply personal perspective on
resilience through generations. The author's journey from
Poland to the United States is a moving account of survival,
courage, and a yearning for freedom. Her storytelling vividly
captures the struggles of her ancestors, her parents' courage
during WWII, and her own coming-of-age as she builds a life
filled with remarkable academic achievements, family, and
self-reflection."

—Angelique Khalifa, Ph.D., Toxicologist

"Marysia Tarnopolska Weiss's story raises awareness
about the millions of people who have moved away from
their motherland. So many people, now residents in North
America, have come from somewhere, and have a story to
tell. Marysia describes her native country with such tangible
detail, much like a compelling character development, you
grow into it, you learn and can nearly smell the air where
she is. Her vivid reflection on coming to America shows
the outside perception versus living reality Americans
experience every day. In her deeply sensual storytelling, she
dances with words, opens our eyes and evokes compassion,

where we are invited to go beyond assumptions and ignorance. A book that will draw you in from the first page."

—BE Alink, CEO, Founder and Inventor, The Alinker, and
  Author of *Inventing BE: A Memoir & Manifesto*

"Captivating, inspirational, and timely! In *Resilient Dreamer*, Marysia Tarnopolska Weiss takes us on a journey of the transformative and healing power of resilience, courage, kindness, and love. This is a must-read for anyone who needs a mega-dose of inspiration, a renewed sense of empowerment, and the courage to keep dreaming!"

—Keiya K Rayne, CEO, Success Attraction Coaching, Spiritual
  Advisor & TEDx Speaker

CONTENTS

Dedication

To all immigrants, past, present, and future.

Acknowledgments

My family is my ultimate dream! I want to thank my loving and loyal husband, Stuart, who has supported my every endeavor for over fifty years. To this day, we dream together.

Thank you to my wonderful kids, who also had their say in this story: Adam, Stefan, Stuie and Mish (Marysia). I am a better person because of all of you. Sometimes motherhood was the ultimate test of resilience, and I know I pushed you all...a little. Thank you to their spouses who made this family complete: Patricia, Dimps, Kate and John. And to our darling grandchildren who brighten and lighten our days: Cassidy, Talulah, Maddie, Xavier, David, Dexter, Penelope, Ryder, Piper, and Gracie.

Thank you to my niece, Magda, for enriching our lives and participating in this book. Her insights provided historical and cultural details from our homeland of Poland. She, too, became a proud American girl.

As I emphasize in my book, friends are the treasures that make this life warm and cozy. Thank you, Pauline and Elli, my friends for 60 years, and Fran and Donna, my friends in retirement whose friendship never wavered. Thank you, Sylvia, who followed me as a math professor and became a lifelong friend.

Thank you, Walton High, for giving me the part of my identity that is purely an American girl and instilling my love of math. And thank you Hofstra University for giving me the priceless opportunity of teaching, leading and mentoring thousands of students over the course of 35 years.

Finally, thank you, Candi Cross, my talented editor for all your insights, encouragement, patience and support for this first-time author. Words are power!

Courageous Crossing

"Every beginning is only a sequel, after all, and the book of events is always open halfway through."

—Wislawa Szymborska, poet

More than 120 million people are displaced around the world because of conflict, climate change, poverty, and modern-day slavery. Some of them willingly risk their lives to touch another border with the hope that it is more welcoming than the land they fled. Into Spain from Morocco. El Salvador, through Guatemala, to Mexico, and finally, the United States for the impossible dream. Thousands of people from Libya escape on the perilous path to Europe each year, with many crossing the Mediterranean Sea from North Africa in rubber dinghies and wooden boats. Others on foot. So many dangerous journeys. They are risking their lives for freedom, perhaps a long-held dream.

As a retired math professor and Polish-American citizen, I often think about all these people coming and going, crisscrossing the oceans for a brighter day. I pray they find what they're seeking, whether safety, education, or vast opportunities their homeland does not afford them.

I think about my own crossing. When I arrived in the United States with my father, Kazimierz Tarnopolski, and mother, Stefania Tarnopolska, I came from Bytom, Poland, but I was born in Opole, capital of Polish song and often referred to as the "Venice of Poland" because of the many bridges hovering over the Młynówka Canal, connecting pedestrians and vehicles to the Old Town and city centre area. Its claim to Insta-worthy fame is the Gothic Piast Tower, dating back to the 14th century. In the Middle Ages, it was one of the four towers forming the defensive walls of the Upper Castle. Withstanding the test of time and battle, it has been called a symbol of Polish resilience. My parents were like the Piast and certainly passed the resilience gene on to me and my brothers.

Following the post-World War II, communist-ruled Poland and Stalin's era, a political recovery allowed a more "liberal" faction, led by Władysław Gomułka, to gain power. By the mid-1960s, my teen years, Poland began experiencing increasing economic and political difficulties. Control over mass media and universities gradually tightened. Censorship of speech, debate, books, raged. As an intellect, scholar, professor, the very thought of censoring ideas and words—access to information and learning—is maddening to me, but my construct of freedom is all-encompassing, thanks to my experiences in Western society.

I remember accompanying my father, Kazimierz Tarnopolski, and mother, Stefania Tarnopolska, to the American Embassy in Warsaw to start our immigration process. There, I tasted my first American cookie, an Oreo. They were salty in comparison to Polish homemade cookies but carried the sweet taste of a better life. In 1966 communist Poland, orange juice was also a luxury, and during those visits, I could enjoy numerous glasses of them for "free".

Leaving Poland behind, we flew KLM through Amsterdam, where we had to stay overnight. I was sixteen years old, on my first airplane, and my anticipation crackling under teenage skin could not be contained! We were heading to the United States...correction, *New York City*, which seemed like another planet by the pictures in magazines—a glitzy machine that produced nonstop electricity (literally and figuratively), style, stardom, hope for all its arrivals. Especially teenage girls, I liked to think.

The crew on KLM was wonderful. They got a kick out of this resilient dreamer sprinting from one side of the plane to another, squealing with excitement as we were landing in Amsterdam. I loved the red roofs of Amsterdam and the feeling of a descending plane. We stayed in a hotel for one night in Amsterdam. Some Polish-speaking lady led us on an evening tour of the city, and I remember observing how the young girls dressed in the West. I was wearing a grey woolen skirt and black fishnet stockings, which I thought were stylish. I noticed that none of the young girls in Amsterdam had black stockings and suddenly, I felt self-conscious and out of style. Nonetheless, my excitement was not diminished. I hardly slept that night. It's as if the flashing lights of Times

Square had already telepathed my key to New York! My brain stayed lit like the city that never sleeps but always dreams.

What dreams did this new country hold for me and my family, however? What would it take to make it after leaving a part of the world enmeshed in turmoil? We didn't even have the language to decipher it all yet.

I would quickly fall in love with America. In addition to its fascinating population representing various cultures, there was the structure of the government, which I found so appealing. No *dictatorship!* Three independent branches of government. *Checks and balances of power!* Religious freedom. *Separation of church and state!* I'm ready to celebrate red, white and blue Independence Day and apple pie—give me a star-spangled banner by dawn's early light and a spoon! I wanted to be part of this world and devour the best parts of it. I wanted my American dream. I would have that dream: education, an academic career, love and marriage, a family. Simultaneously, I would navigate the complexities of identity, carrying the traditions and traumas of my home country while connecting to my authentic self and helping others up in my profession, mathematics—a beautiful, exclusive universe of numbers and symbols— against a wide gender gap. In addition, the structures I ran to as a dreamy teen are hanging on by a thread today, sending me in deep contemplation. What happens to a woman in pursuit of the American dream? Would resilience help pull her through? The ultimate equation! Well, I love words and numbers. Surely, there must be an answer to this problem. As mathematician Sofia Kovalevskaya said, "It is impossible to be a mathematician without being a poet in soul."

She also said, "Say what you know, do what you must, come what may." I follow wise women, so let's do this. It is an honor to share my story with you.

—Marysia Tarnopolska Weiss

CHAPTER 1

Intergenerational Resilience

"There are mysteries, secret zones in each individual."

—Krzysztof Kieslowski, director

Resilience runs in the family like blue eyes and blond hair.

My grandmother, Magdalena Mikluszka, was Polish, and grandfather, Jan Nahulak, was of Hungarian descent. They got married when Magdalena was fifteen and had six children by the time she was thirty. They left three children in care of relatives and in 1913, along with many Eastern Europeans, set out for the U.S. in search of more possibilities. They had three more children born in New York City, including my mom, the fifth child of Magdalena and Jan, born in 1918. This was the era of World War I, so they could not go back to collect their other children left behind in Poland.

By 1922, they felt sufficiently established to return to Eastern Poland. My grandfather stayed in the U.S. while my grandmother took the long journey with three American-born children. Shortly after her arrival, my grandmother died of either typhoid fever or pneumonia, leaving all six children to be orphans in Poland.

Apparently, my grandfather did not take immediate action to reunite with his children. My Aunt Mary and my mom, ages 6 and 4, were placed in an orphanage in Bialy Kamien, operated by Polish Catholic nuns. The nuns were strict and often cruel. Punishment was kneeling on dried peas or getting smashed with a broom. However, the girls received a good education. They were taught proper manners and domestic skills, such as cooking, knitting, embroidery, and sewing. Legend lives in stories, and the Nahulak sisters were avid readers. The nuns had to approve all the reading material, however—censorship before it was en vogue, so to speak. The girls were forbidden to share a bed. My mom was one of the youngest children and she was sometimes cold and frightened, so she would sneak into her sister's bed, risking being punished if caught. The nuns also changed the girls' names, so my mom was now "Teresa" and my aunt Mary, "Basia". It was never clear why they changed names. My educated guess was that they aimed to strip the orphans of their original identities, make them bare without past customs and behaviors, so they might be more obedient.

Eventually, their father's new wife arrived in Poland when my mom was eleven. I don't know why my grandfather didn't travel, complete mystery.

The two sisters shared seven years together in that clandestine place, clinging to each other. Then the

stepmother chose only one of them—Mary—to go back to
the U.S. My mom stayed in the convent, learning domestic
skills, sewing, designing clothes. She miraculously continued
her education in teaching with a focus on elementary school
education to earn a certification, though design and sewing
seemed to be her true passion and talent.

Mary and Stefania wrote to each other frequently until
WWII. Then all correspondence stopped. Through the
Red Cross, they contacted each other after the war and
continued correspondence; their bond never wavered.

Aunt Mary would send us packages. One of her friend's
daughters, Diane, was two years older than I, so I would
get her American clothes that she outgrew. What I found
amazing was that when the two sisters reunited in 1966, they
had the same dress style and organized their closets in an
identical way. They lined up their shoes according to color
as they did their skirts, tops and dresses. Perhaps they still
followed the nun's orderly patterns?

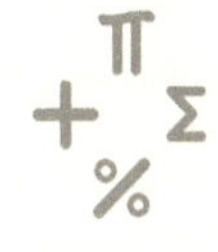

CHAPTER 2

Noble Birth

"No legend emerges from a vacuum."

Because of his father, my dad was considered of noble birth.

Our cousin, Tadeusz Poniatowski, his wife and subsequently, three children, who lived with us from 1954-1960, when the government decided that our apartment was too large for one family, were related to the last king of Poland, Stanislaw August Poniatowski. Of note, Poniatowski, a major patron of the arts who attempted to lead by religious tolerance—my kind of leader—met Catherine Alexeievna, the future empress, Catherine the Great, and they were lovers for decades. He worked on his memoirs, too!

My dad's mother practiced Orthodox religion. She attended church every single day. Grandfather was in the army and died of tuberculosis. The siblings of my father never reached adulthood, perishing to the same fate. My father, a strikingly handsome man using his looks as a playboy of sorts, until he laid eyes on my mom, had a successful engineering-architectural firm and employed over

100 workers before World War II broke out. He was over six feet tall with blond hair and blue-green eyes. His life was luxurious at the time my mom, eight years younger than he, came into his life. This tiny girl, 5'1 with jet black hair, fair skin, and violet blue eyes, spotted my father walking into his office and decided she wanted to marry him! She followed him and knocked on his office door to ask for a secretarial job. He hired her on the spot. I learned from her friend that my mom would actually do a strip tease on his desk. This was the 1930s!

Dad dazzled her with clothes, jewels, dinner parties and servants until she became pregnant in 1939. Well, good Polish girls did not have children out of wedlock. Time to get married! They got married in June of 1939. My mom wore a stylish suit, not the wedding dress she originally designed (which would, many years later, be my wedding dress). She concealed her pregnancy, claiming that her marriage had been one year prior, but I later did the math, and she confided in me about the matter.

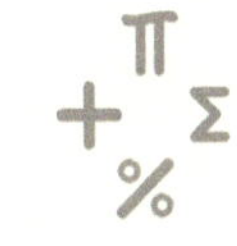

CHAPTER 3
Resilient Country

To measure a country's resilience, we must examine its history, sordid and sensational, heroic and hellish, who its leaders were, against geopolitical and socioeconomic factors. Poland, in particular, has worn many names depending on who controlled it, but its essence remains even today. Through the centuries, juxtaposed with sweeping change at every border, it must be considered resilient. After 1385, Poland and Lithuania had been under the same sovereign. In 1569, Poland and Lithuania united to become a single state under the Union of Krewo, which marked a decisive moment in the histories of both countries. It led to the creation of the Polish Lithuanian Commonwealth, which lasted until the Third Partition of Poland in 1795. It became the most populated country in Europe. The official languages were Polish and Latin.

The government was Parliamentary Monarchy. Monarchy was hereditary during the years 1569-1572. It became elective during the years 1573 till 1791 then Constitutional 1791-1792 and again, elective 1792-1795. The country of Polish-Lithuania Commonwealth was partitioned by Russia, Prussia and Austria. The country of Poland did not exist for 123 years, from 1795 -1918. Three partitions of Poland occurred in 1772, 1793 and in 1795—Poland disappeared from the map of Europe, divided by the kingdoms of Russia, Prussia, and Austria.

Here, you see the rate of change and contrasting reigns, testing the country's resilience perhaps like no other. Nonetheless, Polish language and culture survived. Some credit for the survival is due to the Roman Catholic clergy operating underground educational programs.

Poland lost between 5.5 to 6 million people during WWII; about 3 million of the victims were Polish Jews. So, approximately 3 million non-Jewish Poles lost their lives. Concentration camps in Poland were not "Polish camps"— they were German Nazi camps created to eliminate Jews, Poles, Gypsies, homosexuals and other groups of humanity, who were viewed as inferior or dangerous.

These events testing the resilience of the country ran parallel with the beginning of World War II. My father joined the ill-prepared, poorly equipped, small Polish army. My mom recalled sitting on a hill, seven months pregnant, looking down at my father as the soldiers were boarding the train. He had no training but became an officer because of his noble birth. Crying, she wondered if her unborn child would see his father. Her heart ached; no one had loved her until my father, she told me. Mom moved in with his mother, and they waited for fantastical words of victory together. Victory would be a fantasy because such an outcome was always doubtful under the circumstances.

Inevitably, the Polish army caved in quickly, resulting in mass casualties and injuries, bodies ripped and strewn around the city. Makeshift hospitals were set up, but none contained my father or remnants of him. He was missing in action. Now this pregnant woman and her mother-in-law searched through piles up bodies of soldiers and civilians with their own hands. Finally, they spotted a man in a full-body cast with blue-green eyes peering through. They found him! Wounded but not paralyzed. He had to remain in the cast for months, but with the poor conditions of the hospital room, everyone decided he would be better off recovering at home. They didn't know their house had been destroyed by the bombings. Fortunately, no one was there at the time since their maid was with family in a nearby village. I've thought of my parents' early life with the tragic events occurring in the Middle East, Ukraine, and other places all over the world. One day, coming home to find you have no home, not even the structure of a home.

My grandmother, mom, dad, Josef, his ill brother with tuberculosis, the maid, all crammed into a city apartment. My mom gave birth at home under the care of a midwife, to Adam in 1939. The Germans occupied the city, taking over the remaining infrastructure. I believe Dad's business continued to operate with a business partner. He employed several Jews, who now, had to wear a yellow Star of David, insignia that shouted that they needed to be eliminated. They were required to live in a particular section of town. Not everyone complied. My mother begged my father's secretary, a beautiful blond, who could easily pass for a Polish woman, to deny being Jewish for her safety, which some did, but she was proud of her heritage and refused. She would subsequently die in a Jewish ghetto soon after the occupation. Her sister, Rysia, who looked more Jewish, with black curly hair and dark eyes, sought my mom's wits and assistance to survive.

It turns out that my mom helped many Jewish people at that time. She hid people, risking the lives of her family, who would be publicly executed if caught. Rysia, with whom my mom would later reunite with in the U.S., told me the story of a seven-year-old Jewish girl she saved. My father was still bedridden, so when the Gestapo bamboozled their way into the apartment, they never thought a small child could be under the mattress, where he was laid out, groaning and moaning. My mom obtained Polish papers for the girl and sent her to live in a nearby village.

A lot of these children would need to urgently disappear— she didn't know where these children were coming from or going, but she served as an intermediary. Hair would be dyed, frozen feet from being outside in the cold all night would be dipped in hot water for a minute of thawing. Then someone would come, take the child, change names, and flip them somewhere else. One of my mom's collaborators was a young German soldier, Erwin, who worked in a hospital nearby. He had confided in my mom that in their training the young German soldiers were told that the Jews and Poles were "animals to kill, not human beings", but this conflicted with his heart and knowledge of the people around him, including my mom. He may have fallen in love with her.

A regular Nazi practice would be "catching" the Jews by closing off several blocks of a street and rounding up any Jewish person to be taken to camps, or in some cases, killed on the spot. One time, my mom ended up with several adults fleeing into her apartment. She called Erwin and asked for his help. He showed up in uniform in minutes and paraded them out, claiming that they were his designated Jews to clean toilets at the hospital he was stationed at.

Under the Nazi occupation of Poland, the punishment for helping a Jew was public execution of the helper's entire family. This was the risk my mom took! One night, I asked her what gave her the courage, resilience, and she responded: "How can you turn down a young, pregnant woman about to give birth begging for her life? Others? I helped them because it was the right thing to do."

This all did not pass without many close calls, and she was arrested and taken by a Nazi officer while my father, brother, and grandmother froze in horror. He escorted her out of the building, and she was sure she was going to die. Somehow, he let her go unharmed. She said she bribed him by giving him a very expensive ring. I'm not sure that was enough. Nothing else was said about the matter. But of course, not all soldiers were monsters in uniform. It is said that some were a part of the White Rose movement or other resistance groups who had to play their authoritarian part assigned to them in the public arena.

My brother, at an age as young as 3, was trained to respond to the sirens by grabbing his little suitcase containing some of his clothes and identity information and running to the bomb shelter. I suppose it was like a game for him. My parents were always concerned about him being kidnapped by the Germans. As many as 200,000 Polish children were abducted by the Germans to be adopted by childless families in Germany. The prerequisite was having blond hair and blue eyes. Adam met the criteria, so my parents were ultra-careful regarding his safety.

My brother, Marek, was born in 1944, in a bomb shelter, towards the end of the war. My dad hired a midwife a month before the due date to stay with the family. Hospitals were not safe to deliver a baby. They were operated by the Germans and too often, the mothers died, and the babies disappeared after a delivery. We know one girl who had been abducted, and her father found her twenty-seven years later. Her mother had been killed. She reunited with her father, denounced her German citizenship, and became Polish! Even after the war ended, with Poland in disarray, the hospitals were not safe.

In 1945, Polish families living in the eastern part of Poland had to relocate because the area now belonged to the Soviet Union. My parents had to leave their home with only suitcases and two young children and my grandmother, due to forced migration. Along with thousands of Southeastern Poles, they were made to board trains—and were among the lucky ones not heading to Siberia. Their train took them to Southwestern Poland, a region that before WWII, belonged to Germany. Trains simply stopped long enough for human beings, entire families, to scramble off and find homes. Every time the train would stop, children with pent-up energy would step out to play and at times, be instantly killed by hidden mines. My brothers, 6 and 1, would stay inside because there were so many deadly incidents.

Stefania and Kazimierz.

Kazimierz.

Stefania, Adam, and Marek.

Adam and Marek.

Opole in Silesia was a town where they were instructed to disembark and find a place to live. My parents always thought they could go back and claim their property, but that never happened, as their hometown was no longer part of Poland. My mother blamed FDR for being too soft, allowing Stalin to win and all but pillage the country.

My brother, Adam, was a surprisingly happy and clever child in spite of the traumatic experiences in his early childhood. He was a natural leader always followed by a gang of newfound friends. Marek was not a happy-go-lucky boy. He followed Adam everywhere and did his best to be accepted by the older boys. Marek became my grandmother's favorite, and she would feed him copious amounts of sweets to make up for the hole he felt inside. I think he was somewhat neglected by my parents. My mom had two "forced miscarriages" in between 1941 and 1943. Clearly, Marek was not born in the best of times. Not like things were exactly wonderful in 1949 with my arrival, but the family was at least stable.

I roared into the world, surrounded by women—Grandma, midwife, our maid, and of course, Mom. My brothers were sent out to a neighborhood's house. My father was sitting in the living room, waiting. It wasn't an easy birth, but when his mom announced that "Little Doll" arrived, everyone rejoiced.

I came out pretty boisterous and opinionated. Even as a young child I noticed there was something off with my mom. Perhaps she had trouble processing the multiple traumas in her life. I observed that my mother would go from being loving and inspirational to being a raging lunatic. She was so full of contradictions. She would start reading her romance novels, and the world around her could fall apart. She would fall asleep at 2:00 or 3:00 in the morning and sleep half the day because of her reading marathons. I was lucky if someone else was around to make me breakfast.

When we vacationed in the mountains, my mom would stand on a balcony during thundering storms. She loved the sound of thunder echoing through the mountains and the feeling of rain soaking her clothes and body. I used to be frightened that she would get struck by lightning. She loved the drama and the danger of a storm. She also loved opera, enough to invite opera singers to our home and organize dinner parties where they would perform for her and our guests. It was ALL or nothing with Stefania, period.

My father and his new small crew of construction workers and painters would renovate old churches and other buildings. He helped to reconstruct the town of Bytom, where we moved when I was two years old. While we were moving, I remember sitting on my mother's lap in the cab of the truck uncomfortable and tired, and I knew my crib was in the back of the truck. I wished I could be in that damned crib! No wonder I was tired. The steps in our home were very steep and I could not walk up. I had to pull myself up the railing. Every step was a task for my little legs.

We moved into a big, old German house that was divided into three family dwellings. Our family occupied the second floor that consisted of three bedrooms, an enormous dining/

living room, kitchen and a bathroom with two marble sinks, a tub with a gas water heater above, and a bidet. The toilet room was separate. We also had a large garden, where my grandmother grew vegetables and herbs. There was a gigantic cherry tree, which I loved to climb. It was far more luxurious and spacious than an average apartment in Poland in 1950s. This is perhaps why we had many visitors, and my friends would always hang out at my house.

My mother would play up my dad's noble heritage and call me a "countess". Even though she was not a large woman, she presented herself as a grand, dignified figure. Talk about the "executive presence" in women we refer to today—she possessed it without being an executive. My childhood friends remember my mom and her majestic presence.

The pressure of the government wore on my father. They needed the private businesses but constantly made business hard. It caused my dad to drink, and my mom would immediately attack him, thinking that drinking was for the lowly. She would rage on us all, then go outside and be a perfect lady.

There was constant tension. Radios blasted propaganda. We got a TV with two channels. Many evenings, the adult neighbors and my parents' friends would come over, but ultimately, they would not watch TV or listen to the radio. They would just talk, tell stories. I learned that Soviet soldiers were abhorrent to women. I learned about concentration camps, murder, kidnappings, theft in which if the government thought you had too much, you would no longer have it next day. The score of your hard-earned things would be settled to zero if they so deemed.

No one paid attention to me during these times so I was in my own, little world, literally going deeper and deeper inward. I learned to enact a sort of tunnel effect that consisted of making these people very small and distant; if I tried hard, I could make them disappear. I would see them getting smaller and smaller. I now wonder if this was a physical or mental condition I suffered from but made the most of. Until the age of four, Adam, 15 or 16, would include me in all his activities with friends. They kind of made a spectacle of me because I was athletic and flexible, doing tricks and speaking my mind. My brother, Adam, who was ten years older, recalled that I could out-argue him at the age of 5. But since my comfort zone revolved around being with people unbeknownst them, I felt happy and expressive. Alone, darkness would set in.

On Sunday, after church, we would stroll in the park with the rest of the community. I didn't like playing in the sandbox with other children. I didn't like the feeling of being dirty. I was constantly worried about being contaminated, taken away. If I stayed clean, I wouldn't be sick or taken away. In spite (or perhaps, because of) my obsession with cleanliness in childhood, I did get sick often. I had chickenpox, whooping cough, mumps, measles, and rheumatic fever.

When I was 5 years old, I got seriously ill. I recall being in bed for many days that blended into each other. I didn't really mind because I had no energy to move. The sweat would pour down my braids, and I watched the sweat drops moving—feeling nothing. The nurse would come to the house to give me penicillin shots and I barely felt my bottom being stabbed with needles. Also, doctors came to our home to examine me since hospital care was still questionable in the 1950s. My heart raced all the time, and I ran a high fever. I remember feeling total indifference just observing all that was happening through the fog. People were coming and going, doing things to me and talking about me as if I wasn't there.

My dad was working on the renovation of a cathedral in another town and could not get home for two weeks during my illness. When he returned, he looked like a skeleton. What an ailing pair we made! His concern about my survival made him lose 10 kilograms. One evening, the visiting doctor informed my mom that I may not live through the night. I cannot imagine what she and my grandma felt. My mom kept taking my temperature and watched it go up and up. The doctor told her not to give me any more medication, but she felt urgency to do something on her own, so she gave me half a tablet of an American aspirin. My temperature began to drop. She began to panic thinking that I was dying, which she had accelerated by giving me aspirin. But then, my temperature reached a normal level and remained that way. Over the next few days, I began to recover with continuous home care and penicillin shots. Of course, I could not eat much during my illness and I became highly anemic. My hemoglobin levels were so low that the doctor suspected leukemia. My mom began to force feed me raw liver!

Disgusting! She would try to trick me and disguise it under a forkful of potatoes or grains.

In time, I got stronger and fully recovered. However, the doctors warned my parents that my heart might suffer permanent damage. In retrospect, I am certain that I had rheumatic fever due to strep throat misdiagnosed as a common cold.

When I started school, my doctor gave us a note advising that I should not participate in any strenuous physical activity. I never gave this note to the teachers because I felt fine! I wanted to be a normal kid. I think I made the right decision. I participated in all the school sports, like track and field, volleyball, and soccer. To this day, my heart is strong, but I do have SVT (supraventricular tachycardia, a heart condition that causes the heart to beat abnormally fast, usually due to faulty electrical signals in the heart) as a reminder of my childhood rheumatic fever.

Little girls in white dresses would be in a religious procession on certain Catholic holidays, which spread out through blocks of the town, and I was one of these girls. I remember the sense of panic and fear once I lost sight of my mom. Really scary shit! With what is coming out now about intergenerational trauma, this seems quite a plausible way to explain my fears and experiences, maybe something even passed on. For example, sundowning is a syndrome of becoming uncomfortable when it gets dark. If I'm alone in the dark, I'm frightened. My mother was prescribed Ambien for this. In her eighties, she would call me with hallucinations of "little people jumping on her bed". It was the medication. When my daughter had surgery as a teenager, I gave her Ambien, and she saw people coming out of the painting! I have a heart condition, and my doctor informed me that terror could make me have a fatal heart attack, so I'm careful to not let this phobia run rampant.

I must have been about 5 years old at the time. Adults often talked about certain "patriotic" songs and poems that were forbidden by the communist government. Sometimes at a social gathering at our home, the grownups would sing these songs softly. If you sang certain songs openly, I knew that one could be arrested and interrogated. My family always listened to Radio Free Europe at a low volume. I was worried that my mom or dad could be incarcerated for doing so. Everyone lived in fear.

One night after my parents hosted a social gathering, I had trouble falling asleep. I was sleeping in my parents' bedroom where the radio played softly. At midnight, a song came on, which I thought was forbidden. I got frightened, tried to turn the radio off, but I turned the dial the wrong way and the radio blasted like a roar of thunder. My parents woke up to find me shaking with fear and crying out, "I tried to turn the radio off! Are you going to be arrested?" It turned out the song was the Polish Anthem, which was not illegal. My parents assured me that this song was not forbidden and that everyone was safe.

I was always worried that my parents would be arrested simply because they were not communist, and my father was a business owner. There were always rumors of arrests and interrogations of our neighbors. In general, people did not trust each other and any social life was limited to a small group of trusted and like-minded friends.

Sporadically, some government officials would come to our house claiming that my dad did not pay enough tax, and they would simply confiscate anything that they thought was extravagant, such as a TV set or artwork. I had a collection of tiny American dolls from my Aunt Mary. I liked to display them on top of our black grand piano. One time after the tax collectors visited, they were gone. I was truly heartbroken. I could not imagine why a tax collector would take my dolls. I began to think that these government officials were just common thieves.

As a child in Poland, I had little awareness that there are other people in the world who suffered from wars, were persecuted, experienced hunger, devastation or practiced different religions. Everyone around me was Polish and Roman Catholic. For generations, everyone in my family (on both sides) had blue eyes. Most people I knew had blue or green eyes. Of course, everyone was white. I recall an incident in a catechism class conducted by a priest in church. (Religion was a taboo topic in school.) I was one of the girls preparing to receive my first communion. The priest asked, "What nationality was Jesus?"

Everyone in class said, "Polish!" The priest chuckled and asked if anyone had a different answer. I raised my hand and timidly responded, "Jewish?" The kids laughed.

The priest silenced them and said, "Tarnopolska is correct. Jesus was Jewish." I am not sure how I knew the answer, but it must have been either my mom or my grandma who gave me this information. Of course, everyone in Poland knew about the Holocaust. My parents and the grownups who visited our home talked about World War II's hideous crimes all the time. I was aware of the suffering of the Jews during the war, but I didn't know any Jewish people except my ballet teacher.

Adam was a good student and a lot of fun. He was surrounded by a nice group of friends and was well-liked by teachers and classmates. Marek was getting poor grades, and my mom was frequently angry with him. He was very smart, but he hated school and his teachers. He would constantly get in trouble. Adam would get away with his mischief because of his charm and wit. Marek tended to get caught and was punished with beatings. When he was 14, he decided to run away from home. He left with one of his troubled friends and was missing for two days. Two whole days! He returned on his own, expecting a severe punishment. My parents did not punish him. Mom simply said that he put her through hell and warned him never to do it in the future. He never attempted to do it again. I was so terribly frightened and sad when my brother went missing and so relieved when he returned. I couldn't imagine being on my own. As a 9-year-old, I didn't understand his motive to leave our family. Since my brothers were ten and five years older than I, I am not clear as to their brotherly relationship. I think they were close—Marek looked up to Adam, while Adam was protective of Marek. In my own interest so young and vulnerable in this crazy country, both brothers were very good to me and included me in their world whenever they had a chance.

My best childhood memories in our home were the times I spent with my brothers. Adam was particularly good at inventing games with minimal toys available. I loved decorating the Christmas tree with my brothers. Parents were never involved. We would tie strings to chocolate candies in shiny, colorful wrappers and hang them on the tree, doing our best not to taste them until the tree came down after January 6. Occasionally, one of the chocolates would "break" so of course, we had to eat it!

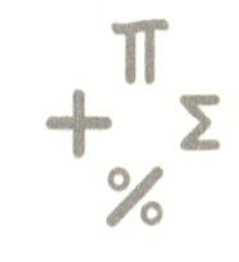

CHAPTER 4

Blue Bike of Bytom

> "Nothing in life is to be feared, it is only to be understood. Now is the time to understand more, so that we may fear less."
>
> —Marie Sklodowska Curie, scientist

Bytom was a coal mining town, surrounded by steel mills, all resulting in nearly unbearable air pollution. If you left the house wearing a white sweater, you returned wearing a grey one. The explosions in the coal mines were not uncommon. I recall my bed shaking during such explosions. No one in my family was a coal miner, but some of my schoolmates lost their fathers or uncles in the mines. The city suffered a great deal of damage during World War II. As a young child, I played in the ruins across the street from our home. There was little parental supervision, so the kids climbed crumbling walls and chased each other in partially destroyed basements. We pretended to be heroic Polish soldiers trying to kill Germans. Miraculously, none of my friends and neighbors got hurt.

When the rebuilding process began, we played in construction sites. I recall the time when my friend and I found a white paste on the construction site and used it like Play-Doh. It was so much fun...until our hands started burning. We ran to my house and scrubbed our hands. Our skin was peeling, but of course, we couldn't tell our parents, and consequently, summon additional punishment. I decided that putting on *smalec* (melted pork fat or lard) was the solution. It actually helped!

In spite of our dreary surroundings, the kids found a way to have fun and pursue mischief. All in all, we felt safe. We never locked our doors, and the kids roamed the streets since there were hardly any cars in the 1950s in Bytom. I learned to ride a bicycle when I was seven. I didn't have a bike, but my neighbor, Elka, who was 10, had one. It was way too big for me, but I didn't mind scabbed knees and shins to gain this skill. I remember the feeling of not being able to reach the seat and the pedals at the same time. Then one day, while I was riding Elka's bike, I saw my mom approaching us with a brand-new blue bike my size. I felt like the luckiest child on the planet. I was the only kid my age in our neighborhood who had her own bike!

In the winter, we had fun in the plentiful snow. We would make snow angels in the middle of the street, build snow statues and tunnels. Spring and fall were magical in Bytom. We walked to school through the park and picked flowers and collected interesting leaves. Often, we spotted the same local pervert in the bushes displaying his penis.

We would point at him and yell, "*Swinia!*" (Pig). I walked to my elementary school with a group of neighborhood kids. We were not afraid of the pervert because he never approached us.

Babcia (Grandma) lived with us since the end of World War II and died when I was 12 years old. She was humble and religious. She wore several skirts on top of each other and modest-looking blouses. In the winter, she would bundle herself in a long wool scarf that covered most of her body as she walked to church every morning for the 5:00 a.m. mass and prayers. Sometimes, as a child, I would go with her, and I would fall asleep next to her in the pew covered by her cozy scarf/blanket.

She was a wonderful cook who could make dinner out of scraps or whatever was in the cupboard. I remember Good Fridays when we were fasting, Babcia would make onion soup with *miszki* (plain ripped pasta made from flour, water and salt). It was delicious and so flavorful! On Good Friday, we were supposed to be somber and prayerful, but I was a girl who couldn't sit still all day. Whenever I would start hopping around, she would say "the devil is getting to you and trying to make you silly on the day that Jesus suffered", but she was not angry with me, nor did she ever raise her voice. I always found that devil part hard to believe, but I didn't argue with Babcia. I argued with my brothers, and I questioned my mom. The latter had painful consequences.

Most Fridays, Babcia made pierogi or potato pancakes with sour cream. I liked hanging out with her in the kitchen.

The cooking smells brought me comfort. I felt safe with my Babcia, because she was all goodness and love. She gathered herbs and made some interesting teas. Other old ladies in town sometimes gossiped that she was a witch. Babcia never gossiped nor repeated gossip. She would just shake her head and giggle if someone bad-mouthed another person, particularly my mom. In the small city of Bytom, where we lived, people loved to spread rumors. The old ladies liked to complain about their daughters-in-law, or their adult children or grandchildren. People said that we were snobs because of our aristocratic name and American clothes (which my Aunt Mary sent us from New York). They speculated that my mom was probably Jewish because both she and my brother, Marek, had black hair. I used that gossip to get rid of an antisemitic boy who wanted to date me when I was 15. When he made an antisemitic remark, I told him that I couldn't date him because my mom was Jewish, and I felt deeply offended. He tried to apologize, but I would not accept his apology.

Babcia and I had secrets. Sometimes when my parents were out in the evening, she would make me swear that I would not tell my parents that she was a secret smoker. She had a long cigarette holder and cigarettes hidden in her closet. She would sit near an open window and while smoking, seemed to transform into a different person. She told me that she had committed great sins in her youth and for that reason, she had to go to church every day. I could never imagine what kind of sins this gentle soul could have committed. I was curious, but she said a child should not know such things. To solidify our secret, she would let me take a puff of her cigarette. I was 6 or 7 years old.

Babcia died in her sleep on January 6, 1961. I was 12 years old. My mom and the maid bathed her body, dressed her in a black dress, placed a rosary in her hands, combed and braided her long, gray hair and placed her in bed. The funeral was to be in a few days. It was cold and the snow was deep. The window to my Babcia's room was left open. I would sit next to her dead body without fear. I dressed warmly and sat by the open window. I watched the wind pushing around dead, discarded Christmas trees, some with silver tinsel still attached. The dead trees made me sad; there was death inside the house and outside.

My friends and I went around town pinning printed posters announcing the death of Ewa Tarnopolska and her funeral. Looking back to her funeral, it could have been a scene from a century ago, a gothic scene—deep white snow and a group of mourners dressed in black walking behind a horse-driven hearse from our home through the streets to the chapel at the cemetery, all against the backdrop of white snow. Mom instructed us not to cry in public and to be dignified. She hated hysteria and public display of deep emotions. Needless to say, gossipers in town blathered that we were "cold" and "unfeeling". The family wore black bands on the upper arm for six months after Babcia's death to indicate that we were mourning a family member, but my mom insisted we didn't have to wear black clothes (as

others did), so none of us did, to the horror and ridicule of
the townspeople.

CHAPTER 5

The Greatest Gifts

"Have a heart and consult your heart."

—Adam Mickiewicz, *author*

One day, when I was 3, my brother, Marek, was playing on the street with a neighborhood boy who had a little sister. He asked this boy if his sister had a friend. She did not, so Marek brought her to our house as a gift for me. He said, "This is Danusia. She lives across the square. You can see her little balcony from Grandma's room. She is also 3, so you should be friends." It was the best gift I ever got from anyone. We became inseparable. Her father was deceased, and her mom worked in the kitchen of a daycare center. Danusia spent more time at our house than her own. She became my sister.

As my brothers got older, they spent less and less time with me. They got involved in sailing and they would spend their summers in the lake area, Mazury, with their sailing club. My mom would take Danusia with us on most summer vacations so that I would have company. Dad stayed in Bytom for work and visited us as often as he could. Mom would also invite her own friend, Maria (pronounced *Marya*, with the accent on the first "a") whom she knew from way back when they were both in the orphanage together (terrorized by the nuns). I called her *Ciocia* (Aunty). She had no children, so whenever we were alone, she would ask me to call her *Mamusia* (Mommy). She would take me to a café and buy me hot chocolate and a pastry of my choice, but I had to call her Mamusia in this setting. She insisted that I not tell my mom, and I never did. Even as a child, I understood that she needed to possess and savor these moments pretending to be a mom.

When I was 7, Adam hosted a big New Year's Eve party at our house. My parents were out at another party. I am not sure where Marek was that evening. Adam and his friends, including his girlfriend, let me stay up for a while. I remember clearly Adam's girlfriend's teal taffeta dress, tightly fitted around her tiny waistline and expanding like a balloon from the waist down to her knees. I thought she was gorgeous, sweet and kind. She put me to bed, and I fell asleep looking at her lovely face. Adam married her a few years later, and they spent sixty years together till Adam's death. (Her name is Marysia, and she lives with her daughter, Magda, in New York).

Marek was a passionate person. He was extremely protective of the people he loved. For example, when I was 15, a young man made a suggestive remark about me. This boy met me in a resort village, in the Pieniny Mountains, a spectacular range with peaks built from weather-resistant Jurassic rocks, mainly limestone and approximately fifteen ravines and gorges. I remember marveling at the sight while this clumsy boy pawed at me. He met my brother when I returned after the summer and uttered with a wink, "Hey, Marek, I met your little sister this summer. She is not a little girl anymore." My brother punched him in the face and broke his jaw!

Later in life, Marek witnessed one of my in-law family members being mean and disrespectful to me. He controlled himself in front of them, but after they left, his eyes welled up with tears as he said through gritted teeth, "I felt like kicking them out of your house! How dare they treat you this way, my sweet little sister!" Marek had difficulty holding his emotions in check, same with his appetite and alcohol consumption. He enjoyed good food and plenty of it. Most often, he drank too much.

He loved his wife, Irena, to the point of obsession. He was incredibly jealous if any man paid attention to her. Anyone flirting with her would put himself in physical danger. Irena worked as a beautician, and my mom was one of her customers before they got married. She catered to my mom, who was a demanding and critical customer. She stopped working outside the home after marriage, but she was sharp and always knew everything about Marek's construction business. In her youth, she had a fabulous, sexy figure, voluptuous breasts, tiny waist, shapely hips and legs. There was something Bridget Bardot-like about her full lips and blond hair, which she often wore up in a sexy bun. My brother thought she was the most beautiful and sexy woman in the world. She was truly devoted to him. She was his strength.

During my childhood and teenage years, Poland was sad, angry and devoid of hope. People seldom smiled when passing each other on the street. Everyone was struggling to provide for their families. Many drank heavily. It was not unusual for us kids to see people, mostly men, staggering through the streets after a pay day. Somber drunkards with bloodshot eyes would gather near a neighborhood kiosk sharing stories of their past glory and their current misery while smoking cigarettes, drinking beer and vodka. It was a normal sight for us as children. I felt lucky that my dad was *not* one of those men.

Polish people felt cheated by the Yalta agreement. A common phrase I heard over and over again was, "President Roosevelt sold us out to Stalin." They felt stuck under the Soviet yolk with no prospects for a better future for themselves and their families. Some people might have been making adequate salaries, but the stores didn't have any goods. I mean literally, bakeries with no bread, meat stores with empty hooks, vegetable stores with potatoes and a few scrappy beets and carrots. Tomatoes, oranges, and bananas were rare to find, and they disappeared as soon as they arrived. Even Krakus Polish Ham was exported and not readily available to Polish people. Rumors would pass in whispers when certain goods were to be delivered.

People would line up in front of stores before any delivery. Of course, there was a way around it, if you could pay off the store manager or were a close friend of one. The managers, in general, would hide some of the delivered goods and sell them to their special customers, often at a higher price. I was a beneficiary of such circumstances because a close friend's mom managed a grocery store. Many store managers would juggle meeting a third of the order for one person, then save items for special customers "under the counter" who would pay more. Just think, a person has given you a job to run a grocery store and you just go by the rules and fixed prices. You get minimal distribution. However, if you've gotten to know the distributor, there are more goods and more profits—no one gets hurt, but somewhere along the chain (retail chain!), the manipulation against the government rules snags. Someone has to pay; someone has to be punished. Two of my friends' mothers went to jail. How did they get caught? Especially if you live in a country where resources are limited, some people may outright or even inadvertently spill the beans for their own handout or break from their own practices being scrutinized. These underground economies still exist all over the world. Surviving is the name of the game.

I recall a particular delivery of stylish shoes. My mom and I rushed to a shoe store. There was a pair of burgundy flats with a pointed front. I was dying to get them. The saleswoman brought the only pair available. It was probably a size too small, but I insisted that they fit perfectly and thought to myself that perhaps they would stretch in time. I was in pain every time I wore them, but never told anyone. In fact, I don't recall ever having comfortable shoes or boots.

No wonder I developed bunions in my thirties! However, my shoes were always as stylish as we could find and admired by my less fortunate friends and classmates. Mom and I shared a love of fashion.

As I got older, my mom remained a walking contradiction of emotions. She treated me cruelly at times while concurrently showering me with love, self-sacrifice and devotion. She truly wanted the best of everything for me. I resented her harsh disciplinary style of parenting, which too often meant getting a beating, but I loved her and in spite of my stubbornness, I needed her approval. She made me strong, independent and resilient. She might have punished me for disobedience, but she never questioned my intelligence and hard work. She would tell me that my superior intelligence is a gift never to be wasted.

I've felt loved and significant all my life. Even when my mom used harsh disciplinary tools such as screaming at me, pulling my hair or hitting me with a belt, I knew she loved me because the same woman was teaching me to observe the beauty of nature, to appreciate music, poetry and performing arts. She took me to my first opera when I was 6 years old. During the summers at the Baltic Sea, we went to outdoor concerts several times a week. She taught me proper table manners and how to walk gracefully. She signed me up for ballet, music and vocal lessons. She told me I was beautiful and highly intelligent. She told me I was an aristocrat, and I must act as such no matter what circumstances I find myself in. She taught me all kinds of domestic skills while saying, in the future when you have domestic help you must understand how things must be done around the house so you can supervise your help. She told me that education should always be my priority.

I recall her declaring, "A woman's life is more difficult than a man's, so you must be educated and *never* depend on a man for your livelihood." I must have been 5 or 6 when she schooled me on these matters, and I thought of my lessons as a secret between us never to be shared with my brothers or my father. I loved school and did well in all my subjects, so I knew getting educated was no problem for me.

My father played a different role in parenting. He never disciplined me; he simply adored me. He had sweet nicknames for me and catered to every whim of mine. I recall one Sunday morning, he offered to make me eggs for breakfast while my grandma was in church, and my mom was still sleeping. I wanted my eggs exactly as my grandma made them. He ended up eating five eggs that I rejected because they were not like my grandma's. Needless to say, my mom would never tolerate such capricious behavior.

When I was in third grade, my dad went to a parent-teacher conference because my mom had another commitment that evening. Apparently, my teacher complained about my behavior, asserting that I permitted other students to cheat off me, I talked to my friends while she presented a lesson and sometimes, I jumped up from my seat and walked around aimlessly. My father asked her how I was doing academically, to which she responded, "There is

no issue with her academic performance, She is very bright."
To this, my dad replied, "It seems that the problem is your
teaching skills. My daughter is a goodhearted girl, and she
likes to help her friends. She is very bright, and you are not
keeping her interest."

When he got home, he brought me chocolates and said,
"You are a perfect student. Keep it up." My mom learned
about my dad's conversation with the teacher a few
days later.

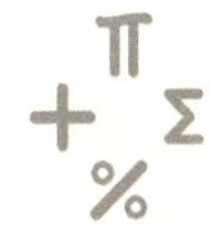

CHAPTER 6

Practice Years

> "I love being a performer. It's like a hole that never closes.
> It's something in you that never dies."
>
> —Dagmara Dominczyk, actress

In elementary school and in the first years of high school, I participated in poetry-reciting contests on a regional level. Some of the poems were about the power of industrialization and the beauty of labor for the common good. It was difficult to get emotional about such topics! When I took the tram with my mom to the competition centers, we passed steel mills and factories. She would point to these structures and call them "beautiful" and "inspiring a bright future". I am sure she did not believe her words, but she wanted to stir my emotions to improve my recitation.

One time, I had to recite a poem about revenge for the Polish victims of WWII. The poet was calling on the dogs of Warsaw whose owners were killed to get together and attack the enemy. After I recited the poem at the rehearsal, my teacher broke down and cried. She said that my delivery was better than any she ever heard. I had tears running down my face as well.

In Bytom and many other cities in Poland, there were Youth Cultural Centers (Mlodziezowy Dom Kultury). All the lessons and clubs were free, but you had to commit. Absences were not tolerated. I took ballet there and belonged to a performance group from the age of 7 to 15. Once a year, my performance group would put on a show using a prestigious venue of Bytom's Opera House, also known as Opera Śląska, where acclaimed soloists Bogdan Paprocki, Andrzej Hiolski, and Krystyna Szostek-Radkowa, and dancers Barbara Bittnerówna and Henryk Konwiński, among others, have graced the stage. The show was usually a fairy tale involving acting, dancing and singing. Our group competed regionally, and we always got first place.

After a few years of training, I was getting lead roles. My mom always helped make costumes, spending long hours creating dresses for princesses, peasants, mysterious girls belonging to a sultan, and imaginative costumes for birdlike creatures, dragons and monsters. She complimented me on my performance and instilled confidence in me, always saying that I was the most talented and beautiful. Our teacher, Pani Bander, was a gorgeous brunette who did it all! She adapted the stories from Hans Anderson, wrote the script, choreographed the dances, chose classical music of Tchaikovsky, Sibelius, Grieg, Ravel and Chopin, depending on the story. She also directed the show. She was strict and demanding, but we worshipped her. Working with our group was her life. She holds a special place in my heart.

In school, our teachers were strict and demanding. We thought of them as the enemy. Most of them were members of the communist party. We wore school uniforms, had to sit straight with our hands behind our backs when the teacher was speaking. The girls who had long hair had to wear braids. Russian language was part of the curriculum from elementary school through high school. The Polish government and its institutions were communist, but most Polish people were opposed to that philosophy and the form of government. My parents and all the parents of my friends despised the government and its "big brother", the Soviet Union.

I was always one of the smartest students in class and someone who attracted friends. I was the leader of the pack, the queen bee. I felt badly for the kids who were not good students. I would let them cheat off me. Exams were never announced in advance. We had to be ready to be tested every school day. We had both written and oral exams. At least three students were called to the blackboard every class for an oral examination. I would mouth the answers to the test "victims".

During inspection, we had to sit straight with our hands place on our desk in front of us. The hands would be inspected, along with our hair. No makeup, no nail polish, no hair style other than simple braids or a short haircut. Everything had to be pure and plain.

In seventh grade, in my new school, I received a note that said, "Will you be my best friend? My name is Basia, and I'm sitting in X row. I've been in class for a week, and I've been looking around for a best friend. I choose you. If you agree, you will know this note binds us." I looked around, smiled at her and nodded yes. I had a best friend, but why not another? Then another, named Wiesia, joined us. The four of us ruled the school—not as mean girls! Far from it. Others relied on us for a lot of things. Now, were we mischievous? Hell yes!

The girls were required to take cooking and domestic skills classes outside of school hours at night, not during regular hours, which were strictly regimented on academics. You had to be prepared at all times, not a day before the test. When you learned something, you had to study it directly after. In the evening, the school was dark except for the boy's mechanics' shop. Some of my friends were not doing that well in their academics, so we would sneak in the darkness to the teacher's lounge, grab the gradebook for our grade and change letters and numbers arbitrarily, even for those who did not ask us to. We made everyone smarter! Now, we were wearing white aprons for cooking where one of us would hide the gradebook.

One evening, after we completed our grade-changing expedition and tried to put back the gradebook, we found the lights on in the teacher's lounge, so we could not put the book back. We brought it to my house, went to the backyard, started a little fire and burned it. We swore no one would know about this. There would never be a "I Know What You

Did Last Summer" movie on this topic, or there would be hell to pay. Everyone promised.

Next day, an announcement came on the speakers that this book was missing. They never found out what we did. Everyone had to be tested, so those who were doing badly likely stayed in that place, unfortunately, despite our efforts.

Elementary school was grade 1-7, high school 8-12. When I was going to seventh grade, my school decided to pick twenty best students and transfer them to high school. I was chosen, but my best friend, Danusia, was not. My mom appealed Danusia's case and somehow, they let her in. My mom, highly empathetic, knew that Danusia was like a sister to me, since I was the only girl in my immediate family.

Remember she herself suffered being separated from her sister, Mary, when they were in the orphanage. Danusia and I cried when the school selected me and not her to start the college prep high school. My mom understood our pain. That's why she fought for Danusia.

My mom took Danusia on summer vacations with us. We would leave Bytom for two months and go to either Pieniny Mountains or the Baltic Sea resort town, Sopot. There, the world-famous Crooked House, a surreal building modeled on fairy-tale illustrations, on the main street, Monciak, was always a friendly, familiar site. Danusia and I were the same size, so she often wore my clothes on those vacations. Her own clothes were not as nice as mine.

In the 1950s and 60s (prior to our immigration), my mom would occasionally get money in dollars from her sister,

Mary. Not sure how the transaction took place, but we had physical American dollars. There was a place where one could legally exchange dollars for zloty, but the rate established by the government was low. Naturally, there was a black market for this exchange yielding a much better rate. With dollars, Poles could buy anything, from imported West German automobiles to Japanese hi-fi sets to French brandy—items not found in ordinary shops.

It's no surprise that dealing with the black market "entrepreneurs" was risky.

The name of the place was Pewex, where you could make the exchange or purchase foreign goods using U.S. dollars, in the neighboring town, Gliwice. One day, when I was thirteen, my mom needed to exchange some dollars, but she was too busy to do it herself, so she gave me $100 in twenty-dollar bills and instructed me to make the exchange. I took the tram and found the place. I wondered about and admired American clothing, such as cowboy boots, shirts and jeans available only if you paid in dollars. I knew not to buy anything. A few customers were around, as well as a salesclerk with an air of superiority. A mysterious man approached me as a sort of wizard of shopping and whispered, "If you have dollars for sale, I can give you a better rate. Step outside." I did. He told me to meet him in the alley behind the store. I was scared but also tempted to get a better rate. He asked me how much I had. I said $20. I knew the official rate and he offered me about 15% more. I agreed and he did exactly as promised. After I received the correct

amount for the $20, I told him I had more and exchanged the
rest. I was shaking with fear as I collected the money and ran
like mad out of the alley.

Once on the tram going back, I was proud of myself and
couldn't wait to tell Mom. She turned pale upon hearing
about my adventure and demanded I never do this again.
She said I was lucky that it was not a government agent or a
criminal who might have killed me.

CHAPTER 7

Ambitious All-American Girl

> "The world is a fabric we weave daily on the great looms of information, discussions, films, books, gossip, little anecdotes."
>
> —Olga Tokarczuk, writer

Aunt Mary, my mother's sister, who came to the U.S. in 1929, was the person who sponsored us when we immigrated to the U.S. on March 7, 1966. We arrived towards the evening at the John F. Kennedy Airport. My mom was an American citizen by birth, so she had received a passport prior to our departure from Poland. My father would be eligible to become an American citizen in three years, while I had to wait five years. Even though Mom was born in New York, I could not automatically become a U.S. citizen as her child because she had not been back to the States since leaving for that long, treacherous journey with her mother before being shoved into an orphanage at age 4.

After being processed by friendly immigration officers, we were meeting Aunt Mary. For some reason I recognized her immediately although this was my first encounter. I loved her from then on. She was beautiful, kind and sweet. My cousin, her son Tommy, drove us from the airport to the Bronx where Aunt Mary lived. On the way, the city lights consumed me. They were everywhere like in my dreams! But I must say I was greatly disappointed in Aunt Mary's dwelling, a shotgun apartment with five rooms in a row, small kitchen and small bathroom with a single sink. It was a lot more modest than our house in Poland.

I asked Aunt Mary where I would sleep. She said that it was a surprise. I thought that some wall was going to open and there would be my opulent bedroom behind it. It turned out that the very couch I was sitting on in their small living room was my bed. I never showed my disappointment and accepted my situation with gratitude. I was brought up to respect adults and their decisions. I would not complain to my parents because I didn't want them to feel unhappy. They had to figure out how our life was going to evolve now.

The only one of Mom's siblings whom I met was my Aunt Mary. Helena, Hanna and Wasyl were born in Slovita, then Austria (later Poland, then USSR, now Ukraine). My brother, Adam and his wife, Marysia, met Helena and Hanna, as well as mom's youngest sibling, John, when they visited the USSR in 1967. Adam recalled an evening when the two sisters sang Ukrainian folk songs called "Dumkas" (loosely translated, "Dreams"). He said they had angelic voices and naturally harmonized. He was transfixed and filled with strange longing, deep emotions—goosebumps and tears. He met both sisters in the village, Slovita.

My Uncle John, on the other hand, lived with his Russian wife, Vala, in a small apartment in Lwów. He was a bus driver who started each morning with two large shots of vodka dutifully set up by his wife. My brother was curious how this man could perform his duties as a bus driver, so one day he went to work with him. Apparently, my uncle continued to consume vodka throughout the day as he picked up passengers on his route. My brother was flabbergasted since this man never appeared to be intoxicated and continued being alert and jovial all day. The apartment was small and as expected, my brother and his wife had very little privacy. One day, Uncle John made a simple statement: "You, my dears, are young, so my wife and I will leave for an hour, and you go to our bedroom and have sex." This direct approach seemed unexpected and somewhat shocking to my sister-in-law.

My brother observed how much more primitive life was in Russia than in Poland at that time. In my uncle's city apartment, without toilets, they had to use an outhouse, while my brother in Poland had a fully functioning, modern bathroom. Also, when my sister-in-law said that she used a washing machine to do her laundry, my uncle and his wife said that they were saying this to spread Western propaganda. They did not believe that such a thing existed. Note that Poland was part of the Soviet block at that time.

Going back to my American experience, a month after our arrival, Aunt Mary informed us that an identical apartment directly above her was vacant. My father took on a job as a house painter so that we could pay our rent and support ourselves. My mom landed a job in the Garment District doing piecework in a sweatshop. This was the first time in her life that she worked outside home. I had my own room in our apartment. When we first moved in, the place was a mess. While my parents went to work, I scrubbed the kitchen floor with a knife to uncover the linoleum under the grime, cleaned the filthy windows and other dirty surfaces. We bought our furniture from Korvette's discount department store, paying monthly installments.

There was an issue with my education. Aunt Mary wanted me to go to a Catholic School, but the school that she contacted required that I learn English first. Eventually, I went to a public high school, Walton High for girls. Before that, I decided to memorize fifty English words a day. Aunt Mary's husband, Uncle Jack, did not speak Polish. He had a serious heart illness and didn't work much, so he helped me with English pronunciation. I stayed with Uncle Jack while the other adults went to work. I studied, cleaned Aunt Mary's apartment and prepared dinner according to Aunt Mary's instructions. She never asked me to do any of those things, but I wanted to be helpful and learn from her. She had a gentle way of correcting me without making me feel inadequate.

Up to the age of sixteen, I never saw a single Black or Asian person. When I came to the U.S. my world changed. It was exciting! I sang with Black girls in my high school chorus; there were Asian, Puerto Rican, and Jewish girls in my classes. A teacher, who had a profound influence on my future, was my mathematics teacher, an Orthodox Jewish woman, Miss Antzelowitz. I made friends easily and soon, my friends were of various races and religions. I loved my new network! It made me feel worldly and sophisticated. Walton High was an educational powerhouse for girls. There, I found my voice, my identity, and discovered my passion for mathematics. A sidebar to my friendships, my maid of honor in 1972 would be a Chinese American friend from high school, Judy Lew, and my bridesmaid would be a Greek American friend, Pauline Sapountzaki.

In contrast, the first years in the U.S. were difficult for my parents. My mom and dad hated their jobs. Having never worked outside the home, she was not used to getting up early in the morning and being surrounded by working-class people. She was depressed, but never showed her feelings to her sister. Her dominant demeanor was gone. Once we immigrated to the U.S. our relationship changed. I was in charge of my parents in many ways. Mom said she was too tired to study English after spending hours working in the sweatshop and enduring the subway commute from the Bronx to Manhattan.

My dad would come home telling us how lazy and stupid his coworkers were. Then my father's personality changed.

He became paranoid and suspicious. He accused my mom
of cheating on him, which was absurd. He began to inspect
my room to find evidence of some wrongdoing. One time,
he found two pills of Tylenol on my nightstand and accused
me of being a drug addict. Another night, he suffered from
a physical episode, which seemed to be a heart attack. We
called an ambulance. He was taken to Lenox Hill Hospital.
After undergoing multiple medical tests, the doctors
determined that he had an overactive thyroid, causing
cardiac issues and paranoia. He needed thyroid surgery. My
Aunt Mary had her work and her ill husband to deal with. I
did not expect her help.

My parents depended on me because I was the only one
who spoke fluent English. I became an adult at the age of
17. I dealt with the social workers in the hospital and the
doctors. They were caring and sympathetic. When I met with
the social services in the hospital, I was frightened that my
father would not receive the needed care because we could
not afford it. The nice lady looked at my concerned eyes and
said, "Child, this is America. We don't turn away sick people.
Don't worry about the payment."

I had to fill multiple forms and sign them for my parents
as their representative. I get touched easily from a piece of
music or someone else's courageous story, but if there is
something to be done, I don't crumble. I step in and do it
without much emotion. I do this without shedding a tear or
being hysterical. The pressure of not speaking English like a
native navigating your parent's medical situation may have

been immense, but I didn't have time to be depressed. I had to act like an adult.

My father received the best of care although we had no insurance. His surgery was successful. We didn't pay a penny. This was America! My father came home and became the normal, loving, gentle and kind man he had always been. We never knew that overactive thyroid could affect your personality with mood swings, hyperactivity and confusion.

Dad started attending night school to learn English. Mom went as well, but she didn't have the willpower to study. My dad studied and asked for my help. His English improved to the point that he landed a job as a supervisor in the engineering department in a hospital in Harlem. My mom quit her sweatshop work. She connected with Rysia, the Jewish woman whose life she saved from the Nazis. Through her, Mom started a part-time job in the Diamond District on 47th Street. She always loved jewelry, so the job was perfect for her.

We had immigrated right after Marek got married. When I returned to Poland for a visit in 1968, they had an adorable baby daughter, Kasia, and Irena was pregnant with their second daughter, Aleksandra. My heart melted when I saw Kasia sleeping in her crib. She looked so much like my brother. That was my primary joy. I knew I didn't belong in Poland anymore. Of course, I will always identify as Polish and I love the Polish language and culture, but this lovely country with its intriguing and often tragic history was just too small for me. Now, I had the world!

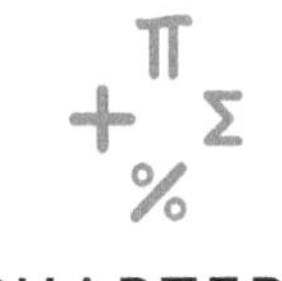

CHAPTER 8

Love Is the Dream

"The first breath of love is the last breath of reason."

–Kornel Makuszyński, children's book author

In 1968, my beloved Uncle Jack died after an open-heart surgery. I would go every day to the hospital after classes while he was in a coma. I recall the day when the doctors said Uncle Jack would most likely die in a matter of hours. Aunt Mary was standing in the hallway near his room as I approached her. She reached out for me and through her tears said, "You came from Poland to be my angel. I don't know what I would do without you."

After Uncle Jack died, I moved in with Aunt Mary. I still had my clothes upstairs in my parents' apartment, but I did my homework and slept in Aunt Mary's place. She was my confidante, and I, hers. We occasionally cried together and cheered each other up.

A year after Uncle Jack died, Aunt Mary's boss, Mr. R., asked her out and confessed that he had been in love with her for years. Aunt Mary did not feel right to go out with him alone, so I became her chaperone. It was fun! Mr. R. took us to the opera and elegant restaurants in the city. I had delightful, costly experiences, which my parents could not afford at the time. At the same time, I started dating Stu. As a college student, the poor guy could not keep up with Mr. R's expensive taste. As college students if we went out, we stopped at one whisky sour each. Having dinner in a restaurant was a luxury. Lunch at a kosher deli was perfect! Having dinner at a diner was good enough.

Aunt Mary and I would talk about our guys late into the night. Stu's family had issues with me not being Jewish. Aunt Mary told me not to give up if I truly loved him. She said, "You might regret losing him for the rest of your life." She said that when she and Uncle Jack were getting married, people told her she was making a mistake marrying a sick man. She felt grateful and lucky that she was his wife until his death at the age of 51. She cherished every minute she spent with him. I wanted this kind of love. And I found it in Stuart Weiss.

Stu wanted to go to University of Alabama and was accepted, but his parents did not approve of his choice, so after spending some time there, he ended up at Lehman College, part of the CUNY system. Math and science were his strong subjects, so he registered for pre-engineering courses, physics and calculus. Going away to college was not an option for me. My parents could not afford it. Although I would have preferred to go to a more prestigious university, I ended up at Lehman in the same physics class as Stu. We had stadium seating in physics. Our professor was from India and had an accent that was difficult to understand. Stu sat in the back row, but I was acutely aware of his presence even though I sat in the front row with my new friend, Sandy. Apparently, Stu was mesmerized by my long, flowing hair (fifty-plus years later, my hair is neither long nor flowing!) but was too intimidated to approach me. Each class, our professor would ask who could solve the homework problems. Most often, I ended up at the blackboard explaining the concepts taught but not understood by the rest of the students because of the language barrier with our teacher. Basically, Sandy and I taught the material to ourselves.

In the meantime, Stu kept choosing his seat closer and closer to the front. One day, he sat directly behind me and after class, our eyes met for the first time. I didn't even know his name, but I felt an electric shock zigzag through my body. I felt as though I recognized him from some unknown past. I sensed that he felt the same. But then, not knowing what to do with this feeling, I turned around and walked out of the classroom with Sandy. From Stu's version, he was trying to figure out how to approach me. Then one day, he noticed a New York Yankees sticker on one of my books. Alas, he had an opening line! None other than...wait for it: "Do you like the Yankees?"

"I am a big fan!" I replied.

He asked me to go to a baseball game, which was a month away. Well, since technically, he asked me out already, I invited him to my birthday party that my friend, Lola, was hosting a month before the baseball season started.

From that day on, we sat in class together. Sandy, Stu and I would have lunch together, and he started walking me to the bus after classes. He says, "In my love haze I would stare at the bus until it disappeared from my sight."

Stu recalls our first date: "My father let me use his old Ford to drive from Queens to Bronx, to pick up Marysia at her home near the Yankee Stadium. I was an hour or ninety minutes early and kept driving until it was time to pick her up for her birthday party. I didn't know her friends. Some were Polish, some Israeli, but everyone except me spoke Polish, as well as heavily accented English. After the party, I brought her home. The brownstone where she lived had a stoop. I had no experience kissing girls, but I made my move. It was a great kiss, but then I slipped off the stoop! She didn't notice, but goofy me left and drove off." It's true, I really didn't notice that he slipped. A first romance will start to block other things out!

Stu also recalls when things were getting serious between us. "Because of the Vietnam War, inflation, high tuition, protests sprang up all over the place. One day, we drove to Albany and walked around, oblivious to the crowds. We held hands and walked into a church, and I remember her saying, 'Religion and your parents will probably keep us apart.' Her words stunned me. But the truth was my parents were vehemently against our dating. It was impossible not to think of a future, the rest of my life, with her."

From the moment our eyes met, we knew that we were destined to spend our life together although we were born in different parts of the world and practiced different religions. We were hungry to learn from each other. In the early years of our courtship, I introduced Stuart to opera and classical music, while he introduced me to rock and roll and jazz. To this day, our taste in music is not identical but we appreciate each other's preferences. We seemed to understand everything about each other, or at least our love seemed to simplify everything. Polish for an English-speaking person is difficult. Every noun has one of three genders: masculine, feminine and neutral. For example, the Polish word for *table* is masculine, *bench*, feminine, *chair*, neutral. Each noun has seven endings depending on where it is in the sentence. I love the Polish language with its nuances based on the culture rooted in thousands of years of development. Stu will never speak this language; however, our own love language superseded the challenges other types of language held.

We got married by a Roman Catholic priest and a rabbi, to please both parents. At that time, I was still a practicing Catholic, so having the blessing of the church was meaningful to me. Stu got a good deal on my engagement ring because my Mom had connections with a dealer in the Diamond District on 47th Street in Manhattan.

Our wedding.

Leading up to these life-changing events, in my
sophomore year of college, my family moved from the South
Bronx to Yonkers. It was a lovely neighborhood. We rented
the second floor in a pretty two-family house owned by a
Polish family. Aunt Mary, now a widow, moved in with us. We
had three bedrooms, a lovely, large kitchen, a dining area and
a large living room. Finally, my parents felt at home in this
foreign land so I could let go of my keen responsibilities to
them. By then, I was definitely an American girl in love with
my American boyfriend, my future husband.

My next visit to Poland was in 1972, just after we got
married. We flew to West Berlin. It was a lively place with
neon lights and porn shops in places that looked like a
mini–Times Square. From there, we took a train to Poland.
As we passed through East Berlin, the scene changed
drastically to darkness. At the entry to East Germany,
people were throwing packages out the windows of the
train and hiding them under the seats. Border security
officers were examining the documents of all passengers,
including us. Extreme tension permeated the air. Stu was
excited like a little boy and feeling like he was part of
a movie. I was less amused. We met my brothers at the
train station in Poznan, known as the birthplace of Poland
with dramatic Renaissance-style buildings everywhere.
There were chickens running around and people sleeping
on the floor. The train station restaurant had a stained
tablecloth. The place looked dirty and shabby, but Stu was
happily mesmerized by the scene. My brothers took us to
a restaurant in a hotel where we stayed for the night. They

slid American dollars under the table for the best meals that could be whipped up in the kitchen. It was an experience for both of us!

We arrived in Bytom the next day. Neighboring stores were out of everything. Nothing had changed by 1972, the same dreary atmosphere. When we got to my hometown, banners of the socialist workers' party were abundant, and Stu snapped photos of it all, drawing unnecessary attention. Every foreigner was a suspect of undermining the Polish socialist/communist government. Stu was totally unaware that he might be in some danger. I was more concerned as were my brothers. We didn't want him to wander out alone. Some memories came rushing back. One former boyfriend of mine was politically involved opposing the government and was an openly practicing Catholic. He had my attention before I flew to America, and there, I had forgotten about him fast. His family was close to the archbishop, who became pope. They operated a famous bakery in a resort town and had two homes. When I returned in 1968, they put me and Danusia up in their home, and the maid would bring in freshly baked goods every morning. They introduced me as his fiancé. He had tried to marry me in secret with the clergy he knew before I immigrated to America, and the idea freaked me out as a sixteen-year-old girl. I didn't want to be a wife! Things were different with Stuart—I wanted to be his forever.

Stu immediately loved both my brothers and their families. We celebrated the baptism of Marek's third daughter, Ania. I was her proud godmother. Right after church, we had a huge banquet at Marek and Irena's home on the outskirts of Bytom. The house was cute, and Irena maintained a beautiful garden. The reception lasted way into the night. When we finished one meal, including dessert, we would start all over again with appetizers, main course and more desert. Everyone was in a festive and jovial mood celebrating our family. My sister in-law did most of the cooking and baking. She was an exceptional homemaker in all aspects. She cooked, cleaned, took care of her daughters, tended her garden where she grew vegetables and flowers. She loved and understood my brother better than anyone. Ania's baptism celebration was Stu's introduction to Polish hospitality. We were not only feasting on an abundance of food, but also swimming in vodka, beer and family love.

By then, Adam had two daughters, Joanna (Joasia), 9, and Magdalena (Magda), 3. Stu said he had never seen more beautiful children as my nieces. My brothers, their families, Stu, Danusia and I spent some time in the mountains that summer, hiking, sightseeing, feasting and drinking. The accommodations were primitive. There was no running water, so we were getting water for cooking and bathing from the well and we had to use an outhouse for other biological needs and torn pieces of newspapers to wipe our behinds. But we were young, healthy and full of the spirit of adventure. We were truly happy and cherished each other's company. Stu and I made love every chance we had on our squeaky country bed.

One morning, Marek said, "I am so jealous of you newlyweds!" Apparently, this country summer house had very thin walls.

Both Adam and Marek married for love and cherished their wives, although they were somewhat chauvinistic in their attitude towards women. Their male chauvinistic attitude did not apply to me. I was *their sister* and therefore, *above all women*! They valued my opinion and respected me when all of us joined adulthood.

Adam was an avid reader and enjoyed sharing his knowledge in various areas with anyone who would listen. He would start by saying, "Did you know that..." But his main passion was sailing. In fact, he even sailed from Poland to Cuba as part of a crew of nine with Polish Sailing Association. He often talked about this spectacular and dangerous trip. In his older years, he tended to live in the past recalling his adventures and travels. Nonetheless, Adam did not dismiss the opinions of younger people even if it went against his beliefs.

CHAPTER 9

Complex Blond Who Solves Problems

"Mathematics is the most beautiful and most powerful creation of the human spirit."

–Stefan Banach, *mathematician*

I chose to study mathematics because of the purity, order, beauty, elegance and clarity it represents.

While in grad school, I was teaching part-time at Queens College of CUNY. I was 23 years old when I walked in to teach my first college class, calculus. It is said calculus puts movement into math, calculating rates of change.

One day, I asked Stu to come and observe me. I wanted to know what he thought of me as a teacher. His answer was, "You are the sexiest professor ever," which was not the comment I was hoping to hear, but I liked it anyway. I was frequently taken for a student. I wore tie dye, bell bottom hip hugger jeans and tight, fitted tops, my long hair often in pigtails. After teaching my two courses at Queens College,

I would run to the bus to go to 42nd Street in Manhattan, where the Graduate Center was located. It was not a nice or secure neighborhood in 1972. I had to walk fast and keep my head down to stay hidden from unsavory by-passers making abominable offers. Regardless, I was incredibly happy. I was married to my soulmate, living in our little love nest in Upper Bronx, studying mathematics, teaching on a college level and feeling so loved, grown up and independent. I saw a bright future ahead.

I started my graduate work while I was still an undergraduate and I decided to skip my master's degree and jump straight to a Ph.D. program at CUNY Graduate Center. I was planning to earn my doctorate in four years, but marriage, two pregnancies and an unfortunate first attempt on my Ph.D. thesis would prolong the process to six years.

I landed my first teaching job as an assistant professor for the spring semester at Baruch College in New York City and subsequently, was offered a tenure-track position for the fall semester of 1979. I also applied for a teaching position at Hofstra University on Long Island since we were planning to move to the suburbs. Naively, I accepted the Baruch offer before I heard from Hofstra and had to renege on the first offer, causing my officemate to curse me out since he recommended me for the position and hoped that we would work together. I didn't realize that he had a major crush on this young, married woman. The same officemate insisted that I "tone down my appearance" and that I was "too pretty and sexy to be taken seriously".

My Hofstra colleagues were very nice to me. In the beginning, they didn't acknowledge my ideas until a male colleague repeated what I suggested, but eventually, I gained their respect. I was the first female with a Ph.D. in mathematics to join the department. There were two older women in the math department, one with a doctorate in education and one who eventually received a doctorate in education. I was also considered the first female researcher to be hired by the department.

I became active in interdepartmental committees such as Curriculum Proposal Committee of Hofstra College of Liberal Arts and Sciences (which I eventually chaired), the Diversity Committee, and many others. I was instrumental in hiring more women and the first African American male to join the math department. Ultimately, I became the first female chair of the math department at Hofstra.

However, most of all, I loved teaching. I taught every course the department had to offer including graduate courses in our master's program (we didn't have a Ph.D. program). I served as a thesis advisor to many students (mostly young women) working on their master's degree. My own research suffered. I was too distracted by motherhood, being a good wife, dealing with my parents' illnesses and teaching. By 1985, I had three sons and my darling daughter.

In the early 1990s again, I returned to research. This time, I dove into a fairly new area of Chaotic Dynamical Systems. After a year of attending conferences (Boston, Stony Brook, Copenhagen, Tokyo) and studying the latest works, I created a course in Dynamical Systems for our students at Hofstra. Later, I guided several students' master's degrees in this area. My publications earned me a full professorship.

I believe I was an excellent teacher and influenced many female students by showing them that a woman can be a mathematics professor, be feminine and attractive, and enjoy life as a mother and wife. Many female students told me that they wanted to be just like me—including embodying the same physical fitness and flexibility. It's true. In the last few years working at Hofstra, I was also teaching yoga in the physical education department as a certified yoga instructor. One of my colleagues informed me that she overheard students saying, "Dr. Weiss is so strong! She was flipping over her students in her yoga class."

My dear friend and protégé, Associate Professor of Mathematics and Chair of the Mathematics Department Sylvia Silberger paints the picture. "We met at a conference when I was in grad school. She saw a talk of mine. We had a conversation, and she encouraged me to apply to Hofstra when I wanted a job. She has been responsible for major things in my life. She got me into yoga. I went to her practicum and did her training. I've been her little disciple, I guess! She represents everything I like. She's intelligent, thoughtful, she has a little wild side, which is fun. Marysia was an incredibly popular teacher, quite well-organized and clear. We worked on a textbook together that I've used several times for the course. As chair, she was approachable yet with an air of confidence and competence. The students trusted her in every way. We have produced many strong female math majors, which Marysia was a big champion of. She is one of the biggest influences of my life. She befriends easily. People hold back a little, and she does not have that self-consciousness. She reaches out."

CHAPTER 10

The Scariest, Most Rewarding Feat

> "Winners are those who have the courage to have
> expectations towards themselves."
>
> —Stanisław Leopold Brzozowski, *writer*

I chose to write about my childbearing experiences because so many young women these days struggle deciding whether to give birth in a hospital or at home. My own daughter chose to give birth at home, feeling that hospitals in the U.S. are not serving women and babies well. I gave birth to my first son at the age of 25, two years after Stu and I got married. I was in labor for eighteen hours, not bad for a first child. The hospital and my doctor did not treat me well.

I intended to have a natural birth without any drugs or anesthesia, but my doctor was impatient. In the final hour of my labor, he sent my husband out of the room. A bunch of medical students came to gawk at my vagina while I was in excruciating pain. Then I lost consciousness and woke up to

be informed that I was the mother of a healthy boy. As much
as I was upset about being put out against my will, I was filled
with joy. As the staff wheeled me out to my room through the
hallway, my mom and dad were waiting there to give me a
hug. I will never forget the look in my father's eyes. He looked
at me as if I performed a miracle.

Stuart was waiting for me in my hospital room. I put
baby Adam to my breast. Tears ran down Stuart's face as he
whispered, "This is the most beautiful sight that I have ever
seen." I was exhausted, slightly disoriented but happy. My
anger towards the doctor was gone.

This feeling of elation did not last when I got home,
unfortunately. The doctor had performed an episiotomy,
cutting me from vagina to anus to widen the vaginal opening.
It was painful to sit and move. My breasts, hard as rocks,
resembled giant balloons. My whole body ached. I was
nursing my baby on demand, so I hardly slept. My parents
lived upstairs in the mother-daughter home, which Stuart
and I bought. We needed their rent to make our mortgage
payments. I could not disclose to anyone how miserable I was
because I was supposed to be happy. I didn't want to wake
up my parents nor Stu. I felt so much abuse to my body. Like
hollowed out. Like others owned my body. Because of my
environment, I thought something was seriously wrong with
me, that I didn't have permission to feel sad or ungrateful.
Here, in a nice home in Queens with plenty of support, how
was I going to ask a woman who had sifted through a pile of

dead bodies with her bare hands to find her soldier husband, for sympathy?

When I went back to doing research and stopped nursing, I felt whole again. I regained control of my body. When I got pregnant again, my mom shouted, "Why again? You're a mathematician! What are you doing to yourself?" But we argued about motherhood on a regular basis. On the day of Adam's baptism, I dressed him in a cute, little white suit. My mom said I did it all wrong, and she took every article of clothing off dramatically, just to put it back on again...in the same manner I did, as far as I could see!

When I resumed my studies and teaching, my mom took care of Adam in my absence, which I will be forever grateful for. It was a pivotal time, setting the course of the rest of my life. I completed my course work and passed my oral exam in Complex Analysis with flying colors, thus, declaring myself a doctoral candidate, and started working on my Ph.D. thesis. I worked on the project suggested by my thesis advisor for nearly a year. Then one day, he called me to his office, looking crestfallen. He informed me that he unintentionally misguided me leading to prove something which had just been shown to be false. At that time, I was eight months pregnant with my second child.

I did not shed a tear, but simply asked him what to work on next. I was determined to obtain my degree. It took me another year to produce Number Theoretical results using complex analysis, which were published as two papers in *Transactions of the American Mathematical Society*. I had to submit my work for publication quickly since another mathematician in France was working on the same subject. Once someone else publishes the work that you have been working on, your work becomes invalid. I defended my work without a glitch and now, I had a doctoral title. This happened in January of 1978. I was also a mom of two healthy boys, Adam Casimir and Stefan Robert.

I gave birth in January 1977 to our second beautiful boy, Stefan. This time, the birth was easy. I was two weeks overdue, so my new doctor and I decided to induce labor. As it turned out, I went into labor naturally on the way to the hospital. I watched the delivery in the mirror, and Stu was next to me holding my hand. I was not drugged, and Stefan was born within thirty minutes of unset of my first contraction. I didn't have episiotomy this time.

Stefan was a peaceful baby and a good sleeper. However, Adam, at the age of two developed night terrors. He would wake up at midnight and scream uncontrollably for at least two hours. There was nothing I could do to calm him down. I didn't sleep much; nonetheless, I continued working on my new thesis topic. Students working on their thesis had shared offices at the grad center.

Sometimes, I would get to my office, lie down on the floor and sleep. My mom found that taking care of two babies was too much for her. My parents decided to move out. I was desperate for childcare, so I invited a woman named Janka from Poland. She was a family friend and sometimes my mom's helper. She was my savior, the kindest and sweetest woman on the planet who genuinely loved my children and took care of them, including basic housework. She had a visitor's visa, but she stayed with me after her visa expired. I defended my Ph.D. a year after Stefan was born, January 1978.

I began teaching at Hofstra in September 1978. We moved to the affluent suburbs, Manhasset, on Long Island. We were the youngest couple on our street, and I must have been the only woman in town who was not a stay-at-home mom. I tried to fit in. We even joined a country club, although I was not a golfer. We moved to Manhasset because of its excellent public schools. We got more of a wakeup call than anything else. Stu was the only Jew at out country club except for another member who was a doctor. We joined this club in our twenties. In the beginning, we were proud of ourselves, but these people did not make us feel good. We lived in an Irish Catholic neighborhood, and everyone belonged to the club. One day, Stu went into the men's grill, sat down at the bar to order a drink, and he was the only person to "order" a drink because all the other men had their "regular" drinks flowing and brought to them. There were several other incidences that made us feel uncomfortable and unwelcome at that country club.

In May 1980, our darling Stuie Zbigniew (middle name meaning "one who defeats anger") was born. He was delivered by a drunk doctor in a tuxedo. The umbilical cord was wrapped around his neck, and he was turning blue, but after a few slaps in the butt, he let out a mighty cry. Later, everybody in the maternity ward was getting their babies, and I didn't get Stuie. I started meandering around the hallway and saw a baby cart just sitting there. Whose baby is that? I lifted him up and took him to my room. Okay, he happened to be Stuie! But where was security? I hope this doesn't happen in hospitals anymore.

He was a good baby. He loved to place himself between Stu and me in bed, grab our noses and smile at both of us.

We had some troubles with childcare after Janka left for Poland, but her nephew's wife, Zuzia, came from Poland to rescue us. After Zuzia came Zosia, Janka's niece, then Teresa, Janka's daughter, then Stasia, Janka's niece, then Marysia, Janka's other nephew's wife. There were few other Polish women who worked as my housekeepers who were not related to Janka. All the women were like family to us. They were loving and hard working. Most of them were well-educated, but their housekeeper's salary in the U.S. exceeded their professional salaries (such as that of a biochemist) in Poland. They sacrificed their family life, left their children for two or three years so that when they came back, they could build homes with the money they earned. They all came from the village of Nieporaz, near Krakow. On holidays, along with my parents and brothers (who eventually immigrated to the US with their families) they helped to keep Polish traditions alive for my kids with the language, music and foods. Through these mixed-culture festivities, all my kids learned to speak short phrases in Polish, requesting what goodies they wanted to eat!

I thought I was done having babies after Stuie was born. Then in 1983, I got pregnant. I was not happy to be pregnant again, but after the initial shock, I was looking forward to welcoming another baby.

Eight months into my pregnancy, after a tennis match, the pain in my midsection hit me hard. The doctor checked for the heartbeat. And with an unsympathetic look, he said plainly, "The baby is dead." I was astounded. How could this baby inside me be dead? The doctor instructed me to go home, didn't propose any plan or attempt to work on me further. I called Dr. Rosenberg, who delivered Stefan, and he urged me to come right over. He checked the heartbeat, and with a concerned look, sent me a few floors up to have a sonogram. When I returned, he was standing there with open arms and embraced me. These two doctors were drastically different human beings. I still could not get this through my head that I would not be delivering a healthy baby. I didn't want to be awake and see this precious thing not breathing. I got knocked out and never saw the baby. This was my choice, and Stu supported me.

I felt that I was being punished for initially not wanting this baby. Guilt, shame and sorrow were my companions now. My husband was wonderfully compassionate and supportive. I went through the day doing what was required of me, but once the kids were asleep, I processed my crying hour. Stu would sit by me, hold my hand and assure me that we would be okay.

Our boys were involved in Little League baseball and on Saturdays, they played at various locations. The schedule was on the fridge and one particular Saturday, May 20, 1989, Stu was in charge of delivering the boys to their games. I was going to come later to watch part of the game since I was involved in preparing for a backyard family party. Stu took Stefan and Stuie to their respective games at different locations. When he got home and checked the schedule, he realized that he dropped off Stuie two hours too early. There were other little kids on the field that wore similar uniforms, so he thought Stuie would just join his team. When we realized his mistake, we rushed to the field, which was situated right next to a major highway. Stuie was not there. We asked other kids if they had seen him, and no one did. We called all his teammates whom we knew, and no one had seen Stuie. We called the police. They searched the surrounding area without success. We waited. I found myself blaming Stuart for his carelessness. I thought the worst. When the police asked me to describe my son, I recall saying, "He would have been 9 years old tomorrow."

His teammates began to arrive. We were checking every arriving car. The last car to arrive was a family from Japan whose little daughter was on Stuie's team, and there was Stuie! The family made the same scheduling mistake and seeing that Stuie was alone, they took him out to lunch. We didn't know this family, so we never called them while searching for our son. The police questioned the family. They were frightened and confused since they didn't speak English. We were hugging our son and crying together. Stuie cried too and kept apologizing. Poor kid thought that he did something wrong. I couldn't calm down for days and kept checking up on Stuie while he slept. He was such a beautiful, sweet and kindhearted boy.

Stefan was 10 years old when he fell out of the treehouse in our neighbor's backyard. The treehouse was at least fifteen feet high. One of the walls of the treehouse was not properly installed and just gave in as he leaned against it. There was a wrought iron bench right underneath the treehouse. Stefan just missed it. He said that he saw the bench as he was falling and did his best while in flight to avoid it by curling into a ball. Unbelievable awareness of a ten-year-old.

His playmates ran to get me screaming that Stefan fell out of the treehouse and might be badly hurt. A mother's nightmare! My neighbor was so shaken up that she kept calling 4-1-1 instead of 9-1-1. Stefan appeared to be okay, just startled. Again, I spent sleepless nights merely watching him. A year or so later, he went through several weeks of bizarre hallucinatory episodes. Since I knew where he was every minute and with whom, I knew there was no way that drugs were involved. I kept him from school because I knew he could not function normally. We had him tested by a neurologist. He spent a night in a hospital with electrodes attached to his head and the doctors found nothing abnormal. At night, Stefan would say scary things such as, "He is sitting on a throne spinning and saying, YOU ARE MINE!" or "Everything is going so fast, please slow it down." He was too frightened to sleep in his bed, because of the terrifying visions that he experienced. I had him sleep with me to make him feel safe. Then we went on a skiing vacation and his hallucinations stopped as suddenly as they started. This will remain a mystery.... Sometimes I think that Stefan's fall from the treehouse might have had something to do with the hallucinations.

Stefan upholds a keen sense of fairness and justice. A guy came into a pizza place and stole a tip jar. Stefan chased him, knocked him down and waited for the police to come. In Manhattan, he witnessed someone stealing a bicycle and he did the same thing. Retrieved it for the original owner fearlessly.

Of these incidents, Stefan says, "I started doing martial arts, jujitsu, in 1993. I wanted to learn how to use my physical power to protect what I believed in. If someone was out of control or hurting others, I could control the situation. I wear my emotions on my sleeves and am a highly empathetic person. I'm moved by lyrics of a song and start crying. As a kid, I questioned why the world was not always fair, why there was so much cruelty. Seeing injustice was always painful to me. Both of my parents believe in justice. My dad is a feminist, understanding the struggles women go through. I'm sure Mom's career helped him develop these traits too because he is so proud of her. My parents were a role model for authenticity and treating everyone with respect."

Never think that your children are not observing your behavior, hearing your words, internalizing how you spend your time and what you at least appear to think is important in the world as they are evolving their own beliefs and passions. Because of my family back in Poland, I continued to be informed of events and injustices affecting my brothers. I would always talk openly about activism and advocacy.

The majority of Polish people did not buy into the socialist/communist form of government for good reasons. In the 1960s and 70s, the economy was in terrible shape. There were dreadful shortages and high prices of all goods. Initially the workers and the intellectuals were not united, although they were equally dissatisfied with the communist system. All protests and demonstrations that took place in 1970s were brutally crushed by the government. Toward the late 1970s, Poles began to galvanize against the government in a united way, culminating in a formation of Solidarity (Solidarność) in September of 1980, the first independent labor union in the Soviet bloc. In 1980, workers in the Lenin Shipyard in Gdańsk barricaded themselves in the plant staging a strike, under the leadership of Lech Wałęsa. Street protests can be easily crushed, but the government was not about to blow up a shipyard, so using this clever move, the workers forced the government to negotiate successfully without resorting to violence.

However, in 1981, Polish government under Wojciech Jaruzelski imposed martial law, attempting to crush the Solidarity movement. Polish Americans, like myself, organized demonstrations in many American cities to bring awareness to the issue of human rights being violated in Poland. I never intended to be politically involved but my heart ached for my Polish brothers and sisters, so I attended one of the demonstrations in New York City.

I was having a conversation with one of the fellow demonstrators, and people around me started to pay attention. Before I knew what was happening, someone lifted me on top of a truck, and I was addressing a large group of people. From there, my involvement exploded. NBC interviewed me, along with Radio Free Europe, and then overnight, I was an invited speaker at several political events addressing human rights issues in oppressed societies. Local politicians on Long Island, who wanted to boost their support by the Polish community, took photographs with me. Stu and I hosted several fundraisers in our home in support of the Solidarity movement.

Then I received a letter from my brother, Adam, informing me that he had been taken to the police station every morning and made to wait until the evening without any food, water, or explanation. This went on for days, until one of the officers advised him, "Tell your little sister in the U.S. to keep her mouth shut!"

That was the end of my involvement. I am not heroic if my (however righteous) actions put my family in danger, but I am glad that I have inspired my kids to advocate for causes they care about.

Besides crying over songs and shows, Stefan and I have more in common than our moral compass for right and wrong. Stefan has a tendency to stutter and when I was a young girl, I stuttered too. I knew when a particular word would give me trouble, words that started with consonants, so, if possible, I would pull from my vocabulary and substitute the term or preface the word with another phrase so that troublesome word would be in the middle, blended in with other words. Eventually, it went away. Stuttering totally went away when I started speaking English.

Nothing dramatic happened to Adam in his childhood other than a broken finger. Actually, I stand corrected, now understanding how traumatic, even deadly, relentless bullying can be. He did experience a trauma of being bullied by a nasty fellow student in third grade, and he carried this pain with him for a long time. Adam was a very gentle boy, which made him an easy target. Being a victim of bullying changed him and made him somewhat withdrawn. He had trouble making friends in high school. Thankfully, he had his swimming friends outside of school. In college, he came into his own socially. He made friends and became a party dude neglecting his studies. I was tough on Adam for his poor academic performance. On one occasion, when he came home for a break, I told him that he had to stay in his room alone during the visit where he would live on bread and water contemplating his life goals. I desperately wanted him to have a successful academic life since I knew his intellectual abilities. He majored in math, which came easily to him, so he decided he did not need to attend classes. He came home for another break while failing Abstract Algebra. I took him to my office at Hofstra and over a three-day weekend, taught him the entire course. His ability to learn difficult concepts in a short period time is amazing.

This is how Adam reflects on our parenting all these years later: "If we didn't meet our mother's expectations, there were consequences. In a way, we feared her disappointment. The reward for meeting her expectations was her not coming down hard on us! I was the first, and she was trying to find her way as a mother. I have my own law practice now. Growing up in a regimented environment helped me be successful. I try to reward my own children more than instill fear of discipline in them. When I went to college, I went wild for a while because of being under constant supervision for so long. My parents have treated their relationship and intimacy as them against the world. When we achieved something, that world stopped to focus on it. My final say has to include what I witness as a parent: All three of my daughters call their grandmother with math problems and life problems. In her, they don't receive a disciplinarian—she relishes in helping them."

I know I was not a perfect mom, and I can accept criticism and forgive myself for my mistakes. I cannot make excuses or try to explain myself. It is insightful to learn of my kids' assessments of my...shall we say, spirited mothering skills now that they've had a thorough taste of parenting and navigating their careers. I'm glad they weren't there for certain instances, particularly in my terrible thirties.

Everyone knows what terrible twos are about, but terrible thirties? Well, I was one of those women who acted up in her early thirties. When I turned thirty, I knew I was not a girl anymore, but I wanted to hold on to my girlhood as long as I could. It didn't matter that I was a wife and a mother. I became a terrible flirt. I never intended to be unfaithful; I just needed to get the attention of other men. In some cases, my flirtatious behavior was misinterpreted. Needless to say, my behavior annoyed Stu, but he was pretty tolerant, knowing that I loved him only.

We didn't drink much when the kids were young, except on some Fridays and holidays. I was a mom of three young boys when we owned a vacation home, a condo in Hilton Head. We were there on a two-week holiday when we met a young couple from Tennessee. Let's call them Sally and Tim. They actually followed us from the beach to the pool area and admitted to doing so, saying they found our family adorable. This was our last night before returning to New York. They suggested we get a babysitter and join them for dinner. Since we didn't have any adult time the entire two weeks, we were happy to follow their suggestion. Kids safely tucked in, we met Sally and Tim in the restaurant.

In South Carolina, they don't serve liquor past midnight on Saturdays, so we were trying to consume as much as we could before midnight. We were having a great time with Sally and Tim. At midnight, they informed us that if we wanted to continue to party, a private club nearby served alcohol until 2:00 a.m. So, off we went to this club, where there was music and dancing. I love to dance, but Stu is not much of a dancer. One of the local Southern boys asked me to dance and in my intoxicated state, I continued to dance with him for a while as Stu kept an eye on me. Eventually, Stu thought I had enough dancing, so he came up to me and my dancing partner and said rather sternly, "Let's go."

My dancing partner was indignant and said, "Sorry buddy, she is with me!"

I thought it was funny, so I said, "Well, whom should I go with?" Stu took me gently by the elbow to lead me away. The young man asked me, "Does this guy beat you, Honey? I can protect you!"

It might have gotten ugly, but Tim stepped in and said, "This guy is her husband, and they have three kids, so leave her alone." I still thought it was funny...

We left the club with Sally and Tim and decided to climb over a fence to go skinny dipping in someone's private pool. The owners were not at home, so we didn't get in trouble. I can't quite remember how we got back to our condo. The kids and the babysitter were asleep.

All this naughtiness on my part did not go unpunished. We were leaving for the airport the next morning. We were not fully packed, and I was in no condition to do anything. Poor Stu had to pack and get the kids ready. He dragged me to our rental car where I immediately passed out.

We were late, so Stu was speeding on our way to the airport. As luck would have it, we were stopped by a traffic control cop. The cop surveyed the car and saw three adorable boys and a semiconscious mom. He asked Stu to step into the police vehicle where a scary-looking shotgun rested. He asked Stu how much money he had in his pocket.

Stu said $100. The cop said, "Okay, you can give it to me, and I will pay your ticket. Take care of this woman of yours." That was it!

We somehow made our flight without me throwing up. Stu was a saint to tolerate my terrible thirties. I also see that my version of "Knife Fight" may have been a result of that stage, too.

When there was too much tension in the family, I would call a meeting after dinner to encourage everyone to express their grievances, pass fruit around as a healthy snack (killing two birds with one stone) and ask the kids what their problem was, one by one, as group therapy. We talked everything out, so no one went to bed upset. Occasionally, my disciplinary ways went sour. In one scene, the boys were going nuts, and I screamed for everyone to come down the stairs. I opened the kitchen cabinet and tried to hand everyone a knife. "Here, have it out now!" I screamed out of desperation. They looked at me like I was a psycho and freaked out. Maybe in that moment, I was a psycho, but I was terrified someone would be thrown from the stair railing or fall accidently with all this mayhem unless I did something drastic. I'm pleased to say no one took a knife nor did I offer this type of group therapy again. Call it intuition.

Speaking of, Adam's intuition was uncanny. He predicted that I would have another child and that it would be a girl. I was pregnant at the time with Mish but was not aware of my pregnancy. Also, when our housekeeper, Zosia, fell from a table while attempting to clean a chandelier, he looked at her wrist (which looked perfectly normal) and said with certainty, "Take her to the hospital, her wrist is broken right here." He was 10 years old, and he was right!

Again, we thought that our family was complete. Then one evening, Adam turned to me, saying, "You are going to have a baby girl. In fact, she is growing in you right now." That was Adam as a child. He had this strange ability to predict the future.

When I realized that I was expecting, I was cautiously ecstatic. I was just hoping the child was normal. I refused any testing. I was ready to accept and love this child no matter what.

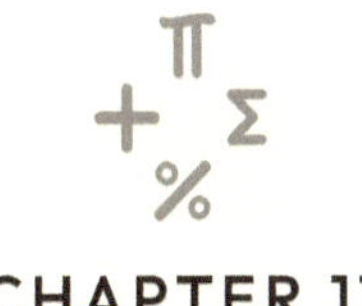

CHAPTER 11

Wonder Women

"It's important to live according to what you feel is right, without pretending you're somebody else and running away from something. When you live like this and you enjoy it, that's when you're happy."

—*Beata Pawlikowska, journalist*

Subconsciously, I decided to buy a pink nightgown and robe as my hospital garment for after delivery. I was rewarded with a perfect baby girl. She was delivered by Dr. Rosenberg, who by then, knew me very well and whom I trusted. I could not believe this blessing. I would hold her, hug and stare at her and repeat to myself, "I HAVE A DAUGHTER!"

On one of the worst nights of my life, my mom was visiting me and planning to stay for a few days. We sat at the table in the kitchen and talked. Mish, age 2, was with us, the boys were upstairs either doing their homework or playing. Stuart was away on a business trip. The housekeeper was in her own room. While my mom and I were engrossed in our conversation, Mish was playing quietly. Suddenly, she

coughed. I turned to see what she was doing, and I noticed
that she opened my mom's purse and was playing with
her pill box. I ran to her and asked her to open her mouth.
Clearly, she had a pill in her mouth. I asked Mom what the
nature of these pills was and how many did she have in the
box, my panic rising. Mom said they were her blood pressure
medication, and she had a seven-day supply with her.
There were only four left, so I knew my tiny 2-year-old just
swallowed three pills.

I don't think my mom realized that my daughter's life
was in danger. I grabbed my daughter and ran to the car. I
drove like a maniac with her sitting on my lap. Fortunately,
St. Francis Hospital was only a five-minute drive. I left the
car in front of the emergency entrance, ran carrying my
baby without stopping to speak to the triage nurses through
the DO NOT ENTER door. There, I quickly described what
happened and showed them the remaining pills. The doctor's
response was immediate. They pumped her stomach and put
her on intravenous fluids. She was so tiny that it was difficult
to insert a needle into her vein. The nurse used a butterfly
needle insertion method successfully.

Mish vomited two whole pills and some fragments. Once
she seemed out of danger, I asked the doctor what would
have happened if I didn't notice that she swallowed the pills.
The doctor said that she would have fallen asleep never
to wake up. They kept her overnight for observation and I
stayed with her. By the morning, she was chipper and ready
to go home. She was discharged and we went up to another

floor to visit my dad who happened to be in the same hospital recovering from a gallbladder surgery. It took me a while to be at peace after this incident. I kept checking on my little girl at night, making sure that she was breathing.

With everyone seemingly out of harm's way, Stu and I decided to be a skiing family and add in more risk factors! Adam was 8 and Stefan, 6, when they had their first skiing lessons at Brodie Mountain in Massachusetts along with us. We are all pretty athletic, so it didn't take much for us all to become proficient skiers. Stefan was a natural and a real daredevil. Adam was cautious. Right after his first half-hour lesson, Stefan zoomed down a hill without holding on to the rope. Adam was not ready to let go. At the bottom of the hill Stefan turned around to see his older brother fiercely holding on to the rope. So, the six-year-old Stefan yelled, "Go Adam, don't be a fucking baby!"

Later that day, Stu and I were on the ski lift and as we looked down. We saw a tiny boy zooming down a not-so-minor hill. I said to Stu, "Look at this little kid, what a skier!" A few seconds later, I yelled, "Oh my God! It's Stefan."

We did not ski at a fancy resort or expect luxurious accommodations. We would stay in one room that was motel-like style at Brodie Mountain, once a well-known New England ski destination. I used to make our sandwiches on the bed, and we would eat our lunch right there in the room. We usually had a simple dinner at the only pub on premises. Stuie was only three so we would leave him at home for a weekend with my mom and dad babysitting in our house.

A year later, Stuie started skiing with us. We went skiing almost every weekend during winter. All three boys became excellent and reckless skiers. They would drop their ski poles from the lift into the forest and ski down between the trees to retrieve them. No one had helmets at that time! We had season passes and every time a skier violated the safety rules a ski patrol would punch a hole in the ski pass. By the end of the season, there was not much left of the boys' passes. They were forever racing and competing and getting in trouble. Stu and I lost control since they were a lot faster than us. They did not participate in many official races since there were only a few such events in this small ski venue. Stefan was definitely the fastest and happy to enter the official race when the opportunity presented itself. He was sure to win in his age group.

Seven weeks after Mish was born, we took her and our housekeeper to Brodie for a winter vacation. We rented a large place that had a kitchen, three bedrooms and a living area right underneath the ski lift. I would ski a few rounds, go nurse little Mish and go up again. I did this all day. At night, we would make a meal and talk about our experiences. On New Year's Eve, the boys would go out in the snow and play football. The teams were Stu and Stuie vs. Adam and Stefan. They played rough and sometimes would come back bloody, happy and exhausted. New Year's Eve football became an annual tradition for several years. As Mish got older, she and I would prepare a little feast while the boys were "killing each other" playing.

Mish started skiing at the age of three. She had tiny feet
so even the smallest ski boots did not fit her. I used to stuff
socks in the toe area of the boot, and she was good to go.
She became a good skier quickly but hated the cold. We
used to put her in the ski school so that we didn't have to be
interrupted by her need to take indoor breaks to warm up.

One winter break, we decided to go to picturesque Mont-
Sainte-Anne in eastern Canada to ski. It was simply frigid,
well below freezing, normal for these parts. I thought it
might be a good experience to put Mish in the French ski
school. She was 5 years old, and she hated every minute of it,
but the rest of us were free to ski uninterrupted.

We were not perfect parents, and we didn't have perfect
kids. During this Canadian vacation, Stu and I chose to have
one dinner out in an elegant restaurant without the kids.
After all, Adam was 16! When we returned, the condo where
we were staying smelled like smoke. They nearly burned
the place down, but everyone was fine and there was no
damage to the place. We never got the complete story of
what occurred. During the same vacation one evening, we
bought tickets for the boys to see a hockey game at Colisée
de Québec, while Stu and I and Mish went to have an
elegant dinner at the enchanting Le Chateau Frontenac. The
5-year-old Mish enjoyed her shrimp cocktail, curled up in a
comfortable chair and fell asleep. Stu and I had a wonderful
dinner and wine. When we left, the hockey game was over.
We had no cell phones, so it was tricky to find the boys. I was
somewhat worried but comforted by the knowledge that they

had each other. When we spotted them alone by one of the exits, I exhaled.

I tried to treat my daughter the same way I treated my sons. I didn't buy her dolls right away and let her play with the toys that belonged to her brothers. She would pick up a monster figure or a transformer and cuddle it, calling it a baby. This surprised me. She was playing a mom without any encouragement or suggestions. She would pick up the blocks and build a home, or make furniture out of it, while the boys were building trucks, tanks and spaceships. Eventually, I let her pick a doll at Toys "R" Us. She picked a Black baby doll as her first doll. (Her biological daughter is half Asian. Of note, there were no Asian dolls available at Toys "R" Us, so times certainly change.)

As a child, Mish was a total girly girl. She swooned over pretty dresses, didn't mind me fixing her hair, posed for photos, and liked looking at herself in the mirror. Her movements were graceful, and she had a beautiful singing voice. She was truly a stunning, little girl, who, in addition to her good looks and sweetness, exhibited a high level of intelligence. She was perceptive and hardworking, always trying to perform on the highest level. I suppose I spoiled my daughter more than my sons. But by the time I had her, I was an older mom and a bit more mellow.

Raising our children in Manhasset, an affluent suburb on Long Island, drove me to break from my newfound mellowness at times. We chose this town because of its excellent public school system. It was a highly competitive town. Most men worked on Wall Street as stockbrokers or investment bankers. Women stayed home, had many babies, volunteered at school and church, and went to lunch. They competed with each other through the accomplishments of their husbands and children. The commute to Manhattan was easy by Long Island Rail Road (LIRR). Express trains made only three stops: Port Washington, Manhasset and Great Neck. Manhasset was mostly Catholic, Great Neck mostly Jewish. Initially Stu worked on Long Island and traveled to various accounting clients in all New York City boroughs, as well as New Jersey and Connecticut. He was (and still is) a skillful accountant with a charming personality. His clients loved him. His income continued to increase, and we lived comfortably. Eventually his office was in Manhattan, a twenty-minute train ride from Manhasset.

I didn't need to work, but I knew that being a stay-at-home mom would make me very unhappy. I loved my family, but I also loved my work. I carried medical insurance for the family, which was helpful, and I was accumulating the maximum retirement pension since my income was not essential.

My mom had been right when she lectured me as a child about women's lives being more difficult than men's. She wanted me to be financially independent. Financial independence has a price. How do you balance professional work and motherhood? Well, the bottom line is that no matter how hard you try, you feel inadequate. Perhaps there are some super women who can do it all and feel good about themselves. I must confess that I am not one of them.

I was too distracted by motherhood to focus on mathematical research. I handled teaching with ease, but mathematical research requires extreme focus. Publishing in mathematics is quite difficult. You must prove a theorem that has not been proven by anyone else in history. Then this theorem has to be deemed sufficiently significant to warrant publication. I was lucky to have an original result published before earning my Ph.D. and having my doctoral theses, resulting in two publications. You must have publications to be granted tenure. I was tenured three years after I got my doctorate, while five years is the usual amount of time. Each promotion requires more publications in addition to excellence in teaching, department and university service, such as playing an active role in various departmental and university committees. It took me a while to reach the title of Associate Professor, but after that, Full Professorship followed quickly because of my return to research and publication.

I lived a full and privileged life, but it was not easy being a good wife and mom of four children, a professor, active member of the university, and a researcher. Never mind running a household. Yes, I had help, but I was the decision maker in every detail: how I liked my laundry to be folded, how and when our meals were made and served, how often the linens and towels were washed, how our beds were made. I did all the grocery shopping because our housekeepers did not drive and moreover, I was the family nutritionist. I drove the kids wherever they needed to go. When we did renovations to our home, I became the project manager. I kept track of all the kids' schedules. I remembered all the birthday invitations and organized the birthday parties for my kids. As my parents aged, I took care of their medical needs by taking them for their doctor appointments, talking to their doctors, and keeping track of their medication. At the end, I arranged their funerals and burials.

Stu helped as much as he could, but his income was substantially higher than mine, so my professional life seemed to be less significant. For years, I never got more than four hours of sleep. How did I feel? Tired! ...And at times, inadequate. Yes, the life of a woman is more difficult.

My boys were swimmers. This sport required intense daily practice most of the year. Often, they had a practice at 5:30 a.m., as well as an after-school practice. Stu helped out as much with driving the kids as his job would allow. Driving to the after-school practices was my job until Adam got his driver's license. I arranged my teaching schedule so that I could pick them up from school with swim bags and snacks already in the car. Their USA swim team used Hofstra's Swim Center's pool. They were training according to age groups, so when one was training, I had the others in one of the classrooms in the same building supervising their homework. Initially, my daughter was training as well, but she was always trying to make an excuse not to go to practice. So, when she turned 8 years old, I asked her if she wanted to continue swimming. She said, "No, but I know I am supposed to because I am a Weiss and the Weisses swim." (Her brothers were becoming known on Long Island as great swimmers, competing on national level in their age groups.) I told Mish that she didn't have to swim, but she needed to find another activity. She chose ballet and theatre. We went to every performance, and we drove her to ballet practices, vocal lessons and auditions.

Our boys had a lot of pressure to do well in school and to compete in swimming. I was definitely contributing to this pressure. I was ambitious for them, and I demanded excellence. "Bs" were not acceptable; losing a race was not an option. Our boys were naturally bright, but they had to be supervised and pushed (maybe too much so). Stuie summed up his life as, "Swimming was such a part of my childhood, all-consuming. She thought it was an avenue to help us get into college. At Hofstra, they had a club team that motivated this, I suppose, and we swam there. I was the best swimmer, having started earlier. I was top ten in the state. I was in the pool all the time. In the winters, we would be swimming. Year after year, until early college, swimming. All friends were swimmers. The only other concern was that it was very difficult to come home with any grade other than 'A'. Not many moms worked. She was an outlier, immigrant, math professor. We stood out! It was like, *why aren't you at home taking care of the kids?* Manhasset was very uppity with old money. They didn't get the respect for being career-driven parents." I can't argue with his summation.

Even with all the helicopter parenting, you don't know which hairpin turns or detours your kids will take. Reflecting on all the milestones along the way of motherhood is simply fascinating.

The summer before Adam's senior year in high school, I started to worry about his adjustment to college life. He was shy and other than fellow swimmers, had difficulty making friends. I didn't want him to be lonely in college, so I came up with the idea of getting him guitar lessons. I figured a guy playing guitar is always the cool guy. He took these lessons over the summer and then started playing on his own, discovering a hidden musical talent. When he started college, he was not only playing guitar, but also singing. As a freshman, he began performing at the Bison, a coffee shop in Bucknell. He majored in math but was never truly devoted to the subject. After graduating with a bachelor's degree in math, he went through a few turbulent years which included a brief marriage, moving back home, taking some post-graduate courses at Hofstra, and finally, deciding to pursue law. While in law school, he met Patricia at a New Year's Eve party organized by Bucknellians. They got engaged exactly a year after and got married a year after that on New Years Eve. By then, he was a lawyer, a musician and composer. Now he has his own law practice, and a rock band in which he is the lead singer and a guitarist. He also taught himself to play piano, just for fun. He enjoys his many friendships and often is the life of a party. He is also a father of three daughters, Cassidy, Talulah, and Penelope. Who knew what would become of this shy boy?

Stefan, on the other hand, was always interested in how things work and why. In high school, he would occasionally neglect subjects other than math and science. Even with our supervision of his homework, Stefan would hide some scientific magazines under his social studies or English homework, pretending to focus on a particular reading assignment, but actually pursuing his interest in science. Without trying very hard he got the highest score in the math achievement test in his graduating class, beating some rather "nerdy" kids who studied like mad. His math talent and achievement, as well as his swimming prowess resulted in acceptance to Columbia School of Engineering. He is the first and only Ivy Leaguer in the family.

Like his older brother, he had some turbulent years after graduating and experienced a brief, unhappy marriage. Fortunately, both Adam and Stefan had no children resulting from their first unsuccessful marriages. Stefan met his current wife, Pearl ("Dimps"), through a mutual friend. They fell in love and ultimately Dimps gave up her dental practice in the Philippines and immigrated to the U.S. to be with him. Now, they have two sons, Xavier and Dexter, both gifted in mathematics.

I refer to Stuie as my easiest child. He never created any problems for us, always trying his best without much fanfare. He is thoughtful and considers the feelings of others more than his own. He did well in high school and in college, majoring in finance. Stuie minored in music and played trombone in his college symphonic band. At Franklin and

Marshall, he met his first wife. They were young when they got married and had two children when their marriage fell apart. Obvious complications ensue when there are children involved. Stuie handled his divorce with admirable grace and poise doing his best to make this difficult journey without hurting the children. He had a very good reason to proceed with the divorce, but he never said anything negative to the kids about their mother. Maddie and David are my precious grandkids who are a product of this failed marriage. They are great and very close with their dad and the rest of our family. Hurt, but not destroyed, Stuie found love again when he met Kate. Kate and Stu are what one would call a power couple, both with successful careers and sharing a luxurious lifestyle. They are happily married and have two children, Ryder and Piper. Kate is a wonderful mom and stepmom.

And there is little Princess Mish! As a student, she showed a lot of self-discipline and determination. We didn't have to push her to work hard. She did it on her own, driven by ambition. In seventh grade, she landed a role of Annie in her school production and caught the "acting bug". She possesses a beautiful singing voice which she enhanced with vocal lessons. She was part of the "theater kids" throughout high school. Her academic achievements, such as a nearly perfect SAT score and her audition performance, earned her a spot in the USC's BFA Theatre program. Earlier, she did a few commercials. After graduation, she stayed in LA, went to many auditions and discovered how difficult the acting profession was. After one terrible experience with a producer, she decided that this life was not for her.

Instead, she earned her master's degree in Chinese medicine and became an internationally known yoga teacher and handstand queen. When she married John Do, they moved to Singapore where they stayed for five years. She could not practice Chinese medicine there because of strict requirements of Singaporean law. Now Mish is back in the U.S. She and John decided to have a baby after ten years of marriage. Gracie is now two years old and the youngest member of the Weiss gang.

Sometimes I think I tried too hard to be a perfect mom and put too much pressure on my kids. How do you learn to be a good mom? I still don't know. One thing is for sure—we loved our kids like crazy and would have done anything to make them happy, healthy, successful, and decent human beings. I think we did okay.

We traveled with the boys to national swim meets. At those meets, they frequently swam morning and afternoon sessions and had to sleep midday. I would close the drapes in the hotel room to create a sleep-inducing atmosphere while I sat in the bathroom making my lesson plans or doing math research. Crazy times!

Over the years, my relationship with my daughter was more complicated than with my sons. We were extremely close all through her high school and college years. While in college, she would call me every day. But then, something changed. I seemed to annoy her. I sensed a resentment towards me. She became critical of all my actions and opinions. This made me sad, and I shed many tears feeling that I was losing my girl to some unknown forces.

We are good now. I know she loves me and respects me. My love for her was unconditional from her birth. Now, she has her own career, and she is a wonderful mom and wife. I think there is something in her that is fighting for her own identity totally separate from me. She often says that she and I are very different. Perhaps we are not and for some reason, she doesn't want to admit it. Without a doubt, my sensitivities toward other women make me more sensitive concerning my daughter.

Ever since I was a little girl, I valued female friendships. All through my school years, I was always a popular girl without trying to be so. I am still in touch with some of my friends who live in Poland. My two closest American high school friends, Pauline and Elli, are godmothers of my children. I met girls in college and in graduate school whose company I enjoyed. I was always a supportive friend and wished all my friends success.

I had not encountered the "mean girls" behavior until I was in my thirties when I joined a country club. I was probably the only woman who was working outside the home. I was quite attractive, had an adoring husband and three athletic sons. My boys would win all the interclub swim meets, so one would think the other members would be happy that the Weiss boys swam for our club. But that was not the case. Female jealousy is toxic. Other moms would openly snub me and gossip behind my back. One told me that it is simply not fair that my sons win all the time since other kids don't train as much as they do. Another mom told me that my boys will not turn out right and possibly get in trouble with the law later on, since I am not there for them when I am at work. Some moms refused to carpool with me. Even the women whom I considered friends said hurtful things to me. One woman whom I befriended at the country club told me that I made her feel inadequate because of everything that I represented.

The club organized triathlons for various age groups of children. These involved golf, tennis and swimming. I was teaching summer courses, and I was not able to witness all the events and did not know the results when I finally made it to the club. I couldn't find my boys right away, but I spotted a friend at the snack bar. I asked her if she had seen my boys. She replied, "What you really want me to say is that each one of your sons is a winner in his age group, right? Well, yes! Surprise surprise." She turned around and walked away. She apologized later and said she was simply overwhelmed with jealousy.

I was not a golfer, ubiquitous in these parts. I played tennis and was good at it. One afternoon, I played a match against a fellow member and beat her 6-2, 6-4. There were no witnesses since it was near dinnertime. After the match, I had to run home, so I asked her to report the results with the pro shop. Later, I found out that she reversed the score, claiming she was the winner. I confronted her and she lied to my face saying that I lost to her. I was shocked!

Currently I am a member of a country club, most of whose members are senior citizens like me. I am a golfer now and enjoy playing golf with our women's group. Most women golfers are very nice and supportive of each other. However, there are a few who enjoy spreading rumors about women by whom they are threatened for some reason. These rumors spread quickly in a gated community and people get hurt. When I first joined the women's group one of the ladies told me, "If you don't like someone, just start spreading rumors about her and watch what happens." I was not prepared to hear this and would certainly not act that way. The same lady invited me to come as a guest to her book club. Being the nerd that I am, I read the book and prepared for the discussion. When not much was being said by the group, I voiced my opinion and asked questions. After discussion ended, the women thanked me for joining them and for making the meeting more interesting. On the way home, the lady who invited me said that the book club filled up, and I would not be able to join. A year later, I found out that she told the other women that I decided not to join because the group was "not intellectual enough" for me. Another shocker!

Each of my friends has lived an interesting, full and successful life. I think of them as "walking novels". I am not in competition with anyone. I support the women in my life and wish them well.

Female friendships are especially important to older women. Pauline, my wise friend of sixty years since high school, says, "When you're a positive person, everything you say sticks. I have this issue with words and language since experiencing brain injury in 2020, and when I get frustrated trying to express myself, Marysia always responds, 'I have the same issue. I forget too! You're great.'"

You see, getting on the same page, resonating with your loved ones, matters.

Even between only women acting in this manner, there would be no shortage of kindness in the world. We no longer feel the subconscious competition over our sex appeal and beauty or accomplishments of our husbands and children. In our retirement, we no longer compete about our own career successes. We just need companionship and understanding. We can laugh about our aging bodies, creepy skin, and encourage each other to feel good about ourselves. We can exchange info about good Botox and filler places. We can lament together about our grandchildren being addicted to electronics and being influenced in a negative way by social media. We can share our need for sex and the fact that our husbands are less able to perform sexually. We enjoy our discussions in the book clubs and documentary clubs. We have girls-only parties to celebrate each other's birthdays. We drink and dance together. Sometimes a female competition sneaks in, but it is temporary like a bad habit that you are trying to overcome. We, married women, welcome widows and divorced women because we know anytime we could be one of them (at this point more likely a widow than a divorcee).

Older women empower each other. With my daughter being 38 years old now, I include her in that echelon. As she is my wonder woman, she gets the final word of this chapter to portray what she feels has been passed on to her and her daughter. Mish says, "What is passed on? My mom's energy, her presence, what she feels everybody in the room feels. This is how powerful she is. I'm sensitive about that power. She dominates, and that can be a powerful quality, she has that sparkle, which I'm grateful for. She's also physically robust. I don't know anyone with that kind of will or sense of self. Her ability to be that is very strong. Her vibrancy would be the quality I'm grateful to have. I did spend several years traveling the world. For five years, I was a wife expat in Singapore. That was a gift.

"I started yoga and kickboxing. Growing up on Long Island, physical strength was aggressive. Rodney Ye, who taught via CDs, had a still presence while being strong. My teenage years drew me to taking care of my body. I moved to LA for college and kept with it. I picked up Tina Turner's book on Buddhism. I always had an orange cat and named one Lotus. I sought inner peace through all these tools. Once I learned physical fitness was more of a result from curiosity, I connected more with inner wisdom than the intellectual. And wow, the inner wisdom of motherhood. The little moments of motherhood are very precious to me. I'm not striving for okay. I'm teaching moms and babies to go upside down, it's excellent for immune system, sense of adventure. It's lighthearted and uplifting. I question how much my time is worth if I'm not with my daughter. A lot of times, it's not worth it to me. I feel very sensitive, and my daughter is a little badass. She's a year and a half and can do a handstand already, does her downward dog, and she knows how to say no in a graceful way. I feel passionate about raising humans that are more compassionate.

"I was living on dopamine hits of excitement traveling the world. Now, I have smooth, gentle highs, a lot of serotonin. For my mom, becoming a woman and teaching me strength was working, having independence, which was hard-fought. I like teaching my daughter that just showing up is enough. Mom assumed I would want the same thing, but it didn't flow like that. I wanted to be there for my daughter. I have less to prove. My mom came as an immigrant and had a lot to do to earn respect from peers. I can hang out with my daughter and feel that's accomplishment enough for now."

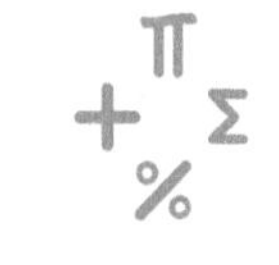

CHAPTER 12

Return to Roots

"Self-respect is the fruit of discipline; the sense of dignity
grows with the ability to say no to oneself."

—Abraham Joshua Heschel, *philosopher*

What are roots? When did they first bloom? I may present
a different take than the traditional definition.

In church, I would pray to God to forgive me for ever
doubting, which I did all the time. I left the Catholic Church
at the age of 50, long after my first sparks of doubt. I tried to
find another spiritual outlet more suited to who I am. When
I started practicing yoga twenty years ago and meditating,
the philosophy of Buddhism appealed to me. We went with
Thai friends to Thailand, and I went to the temple. My friend
taught me that men and women kneel and pray differently,
that I wasn't crawling correctly. Whelp, there goes *that*
religion! I don't gravitate to rules. I tend to believe in past
lives. Something happened to Stu that provoked us to
believe we've known each other in many lives. There is deep
recognition. Ancient roots. Angels.

Stu adds: "I went to the bathroom in the middle of the night, and I saw two angels. Another time, there was an angel over her when I went to kiss her good morning, and I thought she was going to die. I was freaked out all day. That was thirty years ago. Perhaps someone else was simply kissing her good morning too. Thankfully we never go to sleep angry."

When we were recently married and had a second honeymoon in Europe, we were walking around Rome. This feeling came over me as I was taking in the statues. My breath caught, and I turned to Stu and said, "I know you. I really know you. You are him! The one I always loved." I couldn't place how far back, but we both agreed on this long-held connection. Layers and layers. I'm getting goosebumps writing this.

I did a past-life regression and went through two boxes of tissues, seeing my other human experiences. My guide instructed me to keep going down a ladder in my mind. I was Asian and addicted to opium. I was married to Stu, also Asian, and we were attacked. A version of Stefan, my son, carried me out of the battle. Other women were slaughtered. I was so weak from this addiction, I couldn't walk.

Brian Weiss (of no relation), a psychiatrist, who used hypnosis to help his patients, would bring them to their trauma, and some explored their other lives. I had read his books and was enthralled. When Brian Weiss facilitated a session in Manhattan, I dragged Stu to attend the meeting. I tried so hard to go under. I sat there with my eyes closed and focused on Brian's words, but nothing happened. Stu didn't say a word until we left. He looked at me stoically and said, "I saw something." He described his vision/memory: He was sitting with his wife at this long table, and I was a servant. He knew he did something terrible to me. He had a child with me and gave it to his wife, who could not have children.

Stu said, "My goal in this life is to make you happy because of the way I treated you."

Several months passed, and he questioned the validity of this experience. But then we were at a museum, and he looked at some table ware and exclaimed, "That's it! This was on that table." It was from 5,000 years ago.

Our connection to others is so powerful. To me, God is not some all-powerful dictator who decides who lives or dies, who will be lucky and who will suffer. To me, God is the LOVE that connects us all to each other and to everything in nature. God is in everyone and in everything. This is how I think of a higher power, not of something that is separate. Our sense of unity is innate, ancient. I suppose that's my religion.

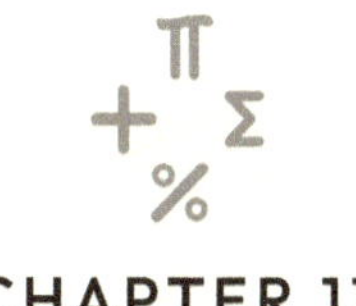

CHAPTER 13

American Dream Team

> "Whatever success I may have attained is due to the fact that since I was old enough to work at all, my ambition has never deserted me."
>
> —Anna Held, *entertainer*

And then there are traditional roots, which are so raw. Immediate family in our tree of life. What do we take from these roots?

When I was pregnant with my first child, someone told me that he and his wife decided not to have children because according to his experience and observation, children end up disliking and resenting their parents. Could this be true?

I loved my parents and always treated them with respect because I was conditioned to behave that way. Did I like them? Did I truly respect them? Was I proud of them? Not always. Had I wished they were different people? Was I ever ashamed of them? Yes, sometimes. My mom had no filter. If someone had a body odor or smelled from cigarette smoke, she would quip, "You stink!" If she didn't like your hairstyle or your body shape or the way you looked at the moment, she would not hesitate to voice her opinion. She had trouble with relationships because she tended to be tactless at times. She would get into verbal fights and lose friendships. I think she simply never developed social skills. I wish she were more congenial. Even as a child, I would cringe when she made inappropriate remarks.

My dad was very much an introvert. He had no friends, only business associates. He was a man of few words. He thought of my mom as someone less intelligent. There was a short period, just before we left for the U.S., when my father drank too much, and my parents fought like crazy. Those were the worst moments in my teenage years. My mom would attack him physically and he would respond by verbal abuse. During some major fights, he would call her "kurwa" (whore). I hated seeing my father losing control. In general, he was such a gentleman. Mom was often out of control, so I was used to that. I suppose the uncertainty over our immigration was a huge stress factor. They took it out on each other.

I wanted my parents to be gentle people. My dad read a lot and was passionate about history and geography. He was a very proud Pole and could give you detailed facts regarding any famous and accomplished Pole (poets, novelists, statesmen, musicians, scientists, mathematicians and actors). In contrast, as stated before, to the detriment of my care as a child, Mom read fiery romance novels.

Yet I know that I am a good person because of my parents. They believed in my intelligence, and they loved me. I attribute any success in life to them. It took me many years to like myself, but I am finally getting there.

I welcomed each of my babies with so much love. I lived through many years of sleep deprivation and anxiety over their well-being. I paid attention to their moods and behavior. I suffered with them when they encountered cruelty from others as teenagers. I desperately wanted to see them happy, accepted by their peers, and successful. I never missed a swim meet, a concert or theatre performance in which they were involved. I rejoiced in their successes, their graduations, weddings, and the births of their children. I suffered through their divorces and was delighted when they found love again.

Every Monday, until kindergarten, my oldest granddaughter, Cassidy, and I would play games, including hide-and-seek. I would turn off all the lights and go around with the flashlight. She had trouble reading, so I would go through flash cards. When she lost focus, I would chase her around the house, two staircases, all around, then when we were out of breath, go read again. She peed in her pants as a toddler, and being old-school Polish grandmother, I would say, "If you do it again, you'll have to go in the garage where there is a gigantic rat!" I own this harsh method and how wrong that was. Now, Cassidy is a freshman in college, and we laugh about it.

My home yoga studio on Long Island became the grandkids' room. Cassidy, Maddie, Talulah, David and

Penelope, my New York-based grandkids, always asked for nighttime stories when they slept over. They loved hearing stories about their fathers and uncles getting into trouble, almost burning down the house after starting a fire in the backyard (Stefan!) and the housekeeper going crazy, running out of the house and hosing it down. They are older now and we are still very close. I also have a deep connection with my California grandsons, whose parents are Stefan and Dimps. Xavier and Dexter are the brightest, most respectful and well-behaved boys on the planet. Dimps is Filipino, yet she embraces some of our Polish traditions and certain aspects of Polish cuisine. In fact, Stefan, Dimps and their sons went to Poland with us to connect with their roots. My sons and daughters-in-law trust us with their children. Stuie and Kate recently left their kids, Ryder, 6, and Piper, 5, with us for a few days while they went on a mini vacation. Gracie, our *tenth* grandchild, doesn't live nearby but we Facetime frequently, and she loves her Grammy and Gramps. Patricia, Adam's wife, encouraged me to write my memoir and connected me with my editor, Candi Cross. My son-in-law, whom I call "My Son John", is Vietnamese and he calls us "Mom" and "Dad". I am grateful for the partners whom my children chose! I adore my daughters-in-law, Patricia, a talented artist, married to Adam, Dimps who sacrificed her dental practice in Philippines to be with Stefan, Kate, the savvy and highly energetic businesswoman, who married Stuie. I cherish my ambitious and successful son-in-law, John. All of our four kids completed their baccalaureate degrees in four years, before continuing their education further. Perhaps there is something to be said for "helicopter" parenting? Twenty of us, our kids, their spouses and our grandchildren, get together for a family vacation at least once a year and enjoy each other's company. They travel from New York, Chicago and California to reunite for a week and celebrate our family.

Daughter and daughters-in-law.
(L to R) Patricia, Dimps, Marysia, Mish, Kate

Sons and son-in-law.
(L to R) John, Adam, Stuart, Stuie, Stefan

Cherishing and celebrating family are essential to me. I called my mom everyday till the day she died. I knew she needed to hear from me. I drove from Long Island at least twice a week to have lunch with her. She was lonely and feeling isolated when my father died. Her English was very poor, unlike my father's. I knew it was my responsibility to make her feel loved. Mom was only 71 when my dad passed away. She was a widow for thirteen years. I took her to all her doctors' appointments, took charge of her medical care, hired a Polish lady who lived in the same apartment building as Mom in Queens to come to her house three times a day, to make sure she ate, took her medications, attended to her personal hygiene, and was tucked in bed at night.

At the end of her life, I found a wonderful hospice with fantastic nursing care. I decorated her room with photos of the family and Polish religious icons. She spent eighteen days there before she died.

I visited Mom every day and stayed for hours (although I was chair of Hofstra's math department at that time and Mish was still in high school). Some days, I would bring Mish to sing to her Babcia. My boys visited her, as well as my nieces. We all showed her a great deal of love and respect.

In this tapestry of life events, I think of Stu's roots, too. His trace of certain traits is not so cut and dry as mine, which I believe makes him even more exceptional because they may start with him. Stuart is ambitious and hard working. He is charming and his charm works well in his accounting practice. His clients love him, and he takes good care of them listening to their financial and personal concerns. I hear him give marital and relationship counseling, as well as business advice. He has one client who is clearly mentally unstable. He is so patient with this client because she has no one to talk to. She calls him at odd hours with most bizarre issues totally unrelated to accounting. He listens and tries to put her mind at ease. He never contradicts her. He has some well-paying clients, but he also does work pro bono or discounts the rate if a client has financial problems.

He is not a saint. Actually, he could be short tempered and moody. I was probably less tolerant and angered more readily at a younger age. Now, between the two of us, I am the more even-tempered. When Stu is not in a good mood, I know how to cheer him up. When he gets angry, I know how to calm him down. He is less skillful in helping me. If I am in a bad mood he gets upset with me. He just wants me to be happy all the time. Clearly, no one is happy all the time. Sadness and anger are normal human emotions. We just have to deal with them without blaming others. I remind myself that most feelings are temporary.

Stu and I love to take long walks. On these walks I often tell him details of a book that I am currently reading. He is not much of a fiction reader, and he enjoys my storytelling. We talk about politics (fortunately, we are on the same page). We talk about our children, grandchildren and our friends. We talk about societal issues and human behavior. He says, "I'm not a guy's guy. I've been to ski trips, and I've been on the phone talking to her. I don't like guys putting down women;

I consider myself a feminist and I've been like that all my life. Even now, guys will make stupid jokes about their wives. I've always respected everything Marysia does. Most men cannot handle strong women. Our relationship is 50/50." What woman wouldn't love this man?

We are surrounded by mostly retired people. Nonetheless, some are constantly in a rush running from one activity to the next. They are impatient on the golf course or waiting for service. Impatience makes one constantly irritated and unhappy. I don't like to feel rushed. Stu says that rushing around is a mindset that does not reflect reality.

Stu and I have always had a very romantic and physical relationship. We've always had an active sexual life. Every day is different, and we try to make it more interesting. So many people are so stagnant, steadfast. We like to experience different settings and witness various lifestyles. After reading an article in *New York Times*, we've rented houses in Burgundy, Shangri-La. We had no idea where we were going or how to get there. But we chose to do it, and our family was fabulously rewarded by an incredible experience of living for a month in the French countryside, surrounded by dairy farms and vineyards. We have been to every country in Europe, Southeast Asia, New Zealand and Australia.

At the age of 62, Stu and I joined a small group of hikers for an eight-day nature experience in Yosemite. Sylvia and her husband Bill, as well as our yoga friends, Lynne and Bill, were part of our group. We hiked about ten miles a day and slept in tents set up for us at various campsites. The

accommodations were primitive. Taking a shower was a
challenge and not available at each campsite. Every night, we
had to seal our toiletries in bear-proof containers, away from
our tents. If you had a biological need at night, you simply left
the tent to relieve yourself nearby, hoping no creature would
find you. It was August, but the nights were cold, so we slept
in woolen hats and mittens. The days were glorious, warm
and dry.

We were well-fed at each campsite at communal tables
where other groups joined us. Dinner was served shortly
after our arrival from the daily hike. After dinner, we were
given two choices for a bag lunch for the next day. Breakfast
was at 7:00 a.m. If you missed breakfast, you went hungry.
Stu devised a plan to have wine delivered to each campsite by
mules. Our group of six would partake in this luxury behind
our tent, like naughty teenagers, before joining others for
dinner. Bill kept a stash of magic brownies for those who
were inclined to partake. Stu never did, but I do have my wild
side. (Naughty thirties, naughty sixties!)

Not everyone in our group made it to the end, but our
friends, Stu and I had no issue surviving. One day, our
wonderful guide had to escort via a shortcut those who
could not complete the trip. We were left on our own to
continue on our trail for the remaining four to six hours until
we reached the campsite. Eight of us remained from the
original group of fourteen. Sylvia was, by far, the strongest
and the youngest in our group. If she led us, we simply could
not keep up. So, I went first, setting a pace, she directed

us from behind me and Stu assumed the last position.
Being surrounded by the most incredible natural sights,
the majestic mountains, the deepest canyons, the clearest
creeks, the lushest forest, the sounds of undisturbed nature
filled my heart with euphoria like nothing else.

Hiking and camping in Yosemite.

I was deliriously joyful realizing how little material things you need for happiness. We each carried our necessary belongings weighing no more than sixteen pounds. Of course, my hair was a mess and wearing makeup seemed absurd. My clothes were far from clean at the end of my trip. Some days, we were physically exhausted. I recall one such late afternoon when I felt I had not an ounce of energy left when we arrived at the campsite. As I collapsed near our tent, our guide called out for us to run up to a plateau to have a 360-degree view of the sunset. I didn't hesitate a second as I magically had enough energy to run uphill to the plateau. The view was truly spectacular and otherworldly. At one of the stops, the guide asked me to teach a gentle yoga class to a group of hikers. I instructed everyone to assume a comfortable sitting position and close their eyes. I asked them to imagine being in a place of incredible natural beauty and then after a few minutes of meditation, I asked them to open their eyes to witness that this was our reality at this moment.

Years later, we took five of our grandkids to Yosemite to hike and bike. I wanted them to experience this natural beauty away from their electronic devices. They were not thrilled every minute, but I am sure they will never forget the trip. Stu and I would allow them to use their electronics after dinner for one hour. Then we would collect them and keep them in our room until the next day. We spent two weeks engaging in outdoor activities. Fortunately, it never rained!

We traveled all over the world and experienced beautiful nature in faraway places, but America's beauty is surpassed by none. Stu and I drove cross-country twice. Each time we traveled at least three weeks taking our time to visit national parks, baseball stadiums, historic monuments, cute towns and major cities and feeling grateful for being citizens of this great country.

Even after fifty-two years of marriage, we seldom pass each other without touching. We are still in love. Is it the same kind of love we felt when we were young? No. When we were young, we took our good health for granted. In December 2023 and January of 2024, Stu had some serious health issues. He had to undergo radiation treatment for his cancer while waiting for a hip replacement. I stopped all my activities to take care of him. He was in a wheelchair when I was taking him for his twenty-eight-day cancer treatment. We would get up at 5:00 a.m. to start the prep for the treatment and head out to the hospital. Strangely, it felt like a lovefest, like we were the only two people in the world in a quest of survival. We must have said "I love you" to each other a million times a day. Stu was totally dependent on me, and I found more love and patience than I knew I was capable of. He is fine now and life is back to "normal".

When we are "normal", we can irritate each other and argue over silly things. It is amazing that one can love a person so much yet find him infuriating at times. Even when we were young and having sex all the time, we would disagree on many issues and have heated discussions. It's a mystery to me why I could look at Stu and think he is the most handsome and sweetest guy in the world and an hour later, find him annoying and unpleasant to be with.

I am sure that Stu dislikes me sometimes, but he loves me always. He tells me that I am beautiful, brilliant, and amazing in every way. He likes the way I smell even if I am sweaty. He tells me that my skin is like silk, and he feels lucky to be my husband.

Overall, we are a close family. We are in touch almost every day by a text thread called "Weiss Gang". There are fifteen of us, since we now include our five oldest grandchildren. Mostly we share our everyday joys with each other. We stick together when facing problems and help each other. Our intertwined roots continue to grow.

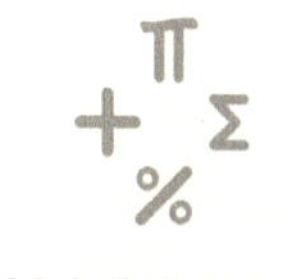

CHAPTER 14

Last Theorem

"Simplicity is the final achievement. After one has played a vast quantity of notes and more notes, it is simplicity that emerges as the crowning reward of art."

—Frederic Chopin, composer

The Department of Mathematics at Hofstra University had been led by men until I was elected chair, making me the first woman chair of this department. When I took over, we had two secretaries. After about a month of working together, these wonderful and conscientious women confessed that they were a bit concerned about having a woman "boss". They heard that women bosses were more difficult to work for. They were pleasantly surprised. We worked very well together and became friends, sharing personal problems and concerns, as well as life's joys. Janice was my senior executive secretary. She was a year or so older than I, and had grown up children, so she preferred to come to work a little later and didn't mind staying until 5:00 p.m. Christine had young children and needed to be home shortly after her sons came back from school. I did not insist that they both work from

9:00 to 5:00. I encouraged them to work out their schedule so that the office would be covered. Most often, Christine was there by 9:00 and left at 4:00 while Janice would come close to 10:00 and stay until 5:00.

Before I took over as chair, the physical office itself was quite unattractive with little space and ugly furniture. I was chair-elect in the summer to assume my position in the fall. Just then, one of the retiring adjunct instructors offered to donate a certain amount of money to the mathematics department under the condition that I would decide how to spend this money. I invited the dean of faculty and the provost to visit our shabby working environment and proposed a renovation project, using the previously mentioned donation and asking the administration for matching funds. I succeeded to get all the money I needed to go ahead with my plan. Walls were moved, increasing our working space and creating a nice student waiting area. We received new carpeting throughout. The secretaries got new desks and chairs, which they chose themselves. I enticed one of my husband's clients to donate comfortable furniture for the student waiting room. I bought a lovely desk for my office with my own money. I also ordered two lovely chairs and a coffee table for my office. I am a strong believer that the aesthetics of the working space contributes to one's overall performance and happiness. Janice and Christine couldn't be happier in the new and greatly improved working environment.

Being in charge of an academic department is not always fun. You must deal with all the student and faculty complaints, help student decisions, run departmental meetings, schedule classes within the guidelines set by the university, and try to honor all the faculty requests. We had a married couple of professors with young children. I would make sure to honor their schedule requests, since as a mom myself I knew the juggling act of childcare.

Janice and Christine made my job easier. They kept my schedule and reminded me of deadlines, they proofread my letters and other statements, they never let unscheduled visitors to my office without checking with me first. When I had to deal with an unpleasant situation, they complimented me for being calm and never raising my voice even if the complainer was acting with anger or was being rude or accusatory. Having Janice and Christine as secretaries was the best part of chairing the department.

I served as an advisor to many students. One of my former students, Elizabeth, showed up at my retirement reception and spoke about her experience. She said she walked into my calculus class, stopping in her tracks. She didn't expect this person for some reason. A woman who acted and looked like me to be a mathematician. She said she wanted to be "that" and chose to major in mathematics. Later, I helped her get a scholarship to Boston University's doctoral program. This same girl said I was straightforward and funny, but I had high expectations of my students. She wanted to do her honors thesis with me. I simply took out a book on chaotic dynamical systems and analysis by Robert Devaney and said, "Read it! Read it and see what you understand. If you like it, I will work with you on your thesis." She ended up doing the very same thing with her students.

I was a normal person with a full life, so the students would also talk to me about their normal problems. One came into my office, gawked at my sons' pictures and asked if any of them were available. A few years later, she married a young man who was tall like my Stuie with other similar features and happened to be of Polish descent. They now have three children and are bringing them up with both Jewish and Catholic traditions.

My female students realized that math could be cool. At the same time, I earned a reputation for being tough yet helpful. Some students found me intimidating especially when I became department chair, but after taking one of my courses, some would ask this "scary woman" to be their thesis advisor.

I am exceptionally grateful for a rewarding thirty-five-year career in an unlikely field for women.

In 1978, when I earned my Ph.D. in Mathematics, only 14% of those degrees were awarded to women in the U.S. Most recent data indicates that about 23% recipients of this degree are women. We are making progress but have a long way to go. I believe that the major reason for male domination in this area of study is the societal attitude. Unlike boys, girls are not expected to excel in math. I had an advantage of going to an all-girls high school where girls were expected to do well in all areas of study. We were not compared to boys nor competed with them. If I recall correctly, at Walton High, all math teachers were females.

The teachers in my kids' school exhibited some of the societal attitudes that favored boys' performance in math. For example, in 1990, one of my son's teachers told a young woman in front of the whole class, "Don't worry about math! You are good-looking and you will marry well."

In 2000, my daughter complained to the principal of junior high that her math teacher used a "dumb blond" joke to illustrate a common algebraic error. Whenever I ask someone to guess what subject I taught at the university, the answer is never mathematics. There is a particular image of a math professor that our society holds, a somewhat crazy-looking man who has trouble keeping eye contact, or a bespeckled, unattractive woman who pays no attention to her appearance. In reality, this is far from the truth.

As a sidebar, the first Fields Medal (math equivalent to the Nobel Prize) was awarded to a woman in 2014. The recipient was Maryam Mirzakhani, a Stanford University professor. There are only two women with this honor. Could bias have something to do with the selection process? The second winner was sphere-packing number theorist Maryna Viazovska (in 2022), a Ukrainian professor at the Institute of Mathematics of the École Polytechnique Fédérale de Lausanne in Switzerland. Both women would be considered as "attractive".

I recall my first mathematical conference in Pittsburg, where I presented my work, "A Remark on a Result of McKean", published in the *Proceedings of the American Mathematical Society*. It was a year before I earned my Ph.D. I was happy to be a published mathematician before earning my doctorate. There were only two women participants at that conference and over one hundred men. Needless to say, I received a lot of attention; some of this attention was professional and some, not so much. I was 27, a married woman with two small children, but being rather small, I looked much younger. The participants stayed in the dorm of the University of Pittsburgh. The school was not in session, so the dorms were empty. I was the only one on the women's floor at night because the other woman was older and chose to stay in a hotel. I was truly scared since I fear being alone at night in the best of circumstances. Of course, one of the young fellow mathematicians volunteered to keep me company, which I declined, and which only increased my fear. Somehow, I conquered my fears and nervousness, presented my work successfully and got home to my darling husband and babies in one piece.

Some of the math conferences stand out in my memory more than others. In the 1990s, I started doing research in Chaotic Dynamical Systems. In every field of study, there are men (seldom women) who are the all-knowing "gods" to whom everyone looks up. This was not different in the area of Dynamical Systems. I met two of these "gods" and both made sexual passes at me. Their technique was exactly the same. At the conference, either during a break or at the end of the session, Professor God would approach me and ask if I wanted to discuss a particular theorem while taking a walk with him in the park or the woods, depending on the setting.

In one case, in the park, Professor God #2 asked if I would like to switch t-shirts with him right then and there. I declined and quickly returned to my room alone, though he suggested that we continue our discussion in his room.

At another conference, a group of us decided to take a walk in the woods. Professor God #1 was next to me and got me involved in a conversation. I was paying close attention to his insightful monologue regarding the last lecture and didn't notice that the rest of the group was far ahead, and we were suddenly alone. He was a much older man and quite famous in the field, so I was flattered that he gave me so much of his attention until he stopped, called me irresistible, tried to kiss me and grabbed me inappropriately. It was the most humiliating experience. I respected this man and looked up to him, but at that moment, I found him most repulsive. Shocked, I pushed him away gently and told him that I loved my husband. He said that he loved his wife too and that this had nothing to do with his commitment to his wife. My response was that my marriage didn't work the same way. He laughed and called me "a silly girl". He behaved as though he truly had the right to treat me that way and I should be grateful and cooperative. I was ashamed to tell anyone about it. These incidents took place before the #MeToo movement. I blamed myself for being naive. I felt stupid for thinking that this man actually found me smart enough to discuss the depths of mathematical theorems.

My story is not unique. Many women of all ages are subjected to the delusional sexual entitlement of prominent and powerful men.

I must admit that I was sexually approached by men at every math conference I attended. I often wondered if there was something about my conduct that prompted this behavior, but I never welcomed any sexual attention from these men. I know that in a professional setting, I never behaved in a flirtatious way because I wanted to be taken seriously as a mathematician. Perhaps I stood out because there were so few women researchers in attendance at the mathematical conferences.

Although I was never raped, I fully understand why women who were violated don't confront their rapists until years later. Everyone has a limit on the amount of pain and shame to deal with at one time.

The year I chose to retire, I taught my favorite class, a two-semester course in Abstract Algebra, the study of algebraic structures. Algebraic structures include groups, rings, fields, modules, vector spaces, lattices, and algebras over a field (I know to most people this is a foreign language). My students, whom I adored, were math majors in their senior or junior year. My final lecture was Galois Theorem, one of the most beautiful concepts in mathematics. Since this would be my last lecture, I called it the *Last Theorem*.

When I was done, the students applauded. As I was leaving the classroom, they chanted, "We love you, Weiss." Tears ran down my face as I walked to my office.

I will never forget the faces of my students. I am still Facebook friends with many of them and I love to see them getting married, advancing in their careers, and having babies. One student who was a junior in my last class said that a few of them had another math class in the same classroom the year after I retired. They would say to each other, "Wouldn't it be great if Weiss walked in one day instead of our professor..."

One couple first met in my class. The class was Introduction to Abstract Math, where I used a manuscript that I wrote with Sylvia Silberger. The young man took the class as a senior math major who needed one more course. The young woman was a sophomore whom he frequently helped to understand the material and to solve the homework problems. On their wedding day, they went to the very classroom dressed as bride and groom and took a photo sitting in the very seats they occupied a few years ago. I am a romantic, so I just love their story.

I retired early at age sixty-two. The dean of faculty was shocked at my decision to take early retirement. At my retirement speech I said, "I just want to have more time. They say, you can't have everything. I think you can have everything, but not at the same time."

Overall, I am extremely grateful to Hofstra University and the mathematics department for nourishing my passion for academic life. I am grateful for all my students who allowed me to show them the pure beauty of mathematics! An appropriate close of this chapter would me what one student wrote in her evaluation: "Hofstra is losing something wonderful when you retire. Love, luck and happiness in the next stage of your life."

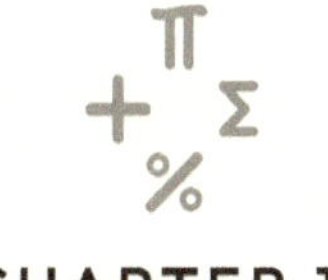

CHAPTER 15

Era of Resilience

"There is no comfort zone. You continue to work hard, to be consistent and to deliver performances."

—*Lukasz Fabianski, athlete*

In casting my story around resilience, a trait that has defined my life, I started with the intricacies of immigration. In truth, the evolution of my plot (i.e. life) may always include it. Therefore, it's worth tying up a few loose ends.

My brothers immigrated to the U.S. later in their lives. They were not allowed to leave Poland with us in 1966 because they were young men of "the army age". My parents were considered useless at their respective ages, 48 and 55, and I, a 16-year-old girl, apparently equally useless to the communist government. Ironically, according to American law, my brother, Adam, born in 1939, was an American citizen (although born in a foreign country) because my mom was American born. Marek and I were not American citizens since the immigration laws changed in 1941.

Marek immigrated in 1978 with his wife, Irena, and his
three daughters, Katarzyna (called Kasia, age 12), Aleksandra
(called Olenka, age 10) and Anna (called Ania, age 7). In
Polish we seldom use the proper "official names". My official
name on my baptismal certificate is "Maria", pronounced
Marya with an accent on the "a", but no one ever called me
by that version of my name. I was always called *Marysia*,
pronounced in English, "Marisha". My friends in Poland
called me "Marishka". No one who speaks Polish would be
confused by this. These are not nicknames. They are simply
variations of the same name. In Polish, I may be called
Marylka, Marysienka, Marishka, Marychna, Maryna, and
everyone would know that my official name is Maria. My
husband calls me "Marysiu" when he wants my attention,
imitating my Polish relatives and using the proper declension
of Polish nouns. All nouns are subject to declensions in
Polish, depending on where they are located in the sentence.
For example, in addition to the other variations, you would
say *Marysi* when you refer to an object related to me or
belonging to me, *Marysię*, when you talk about inviting me;
Marysią if you are enchanted by me.

As you can see, my English-speaking reader, Polish is
not easy to master, but I get enthralled by explaining the
intricacies of the Polish language. I'm not only a numbers girl.
Nevertheless, pardon me, I digressed from my story about
my brothers' American experience.

We picked up Marek's family at JFK. Stu recalls that
their biggest suitcase contained only books. He found

that impressive. When Marek's family arrived, there was not enough space in our parents' apartment in Queens to house them all, so I took my nieces to live in my house while Marek and Irena tried to find their bearings in the new country, settling temporarily with our parents. The girls didn't seem to mind living in our house in Manhasset. We had a Polish housekeeper, so they didn't feel the pain of the language barrier. They also had me, speaking Polish, and the kindest Uncle Stu, who although not speaking Polish, was sweet to them and welcoming. Our sons Adam and Stefan were little, and they enjoyed cousins living with us who spoke the language they were somewhat familiar with. I don't remember how long the girls lived with us. I recall that when we picked them up at JFK, they were wearing winter coats. They were enrolled in school in Queens the following September and by then, they were reunited with their parents in their own apartment. The girls learned English quickly and within a year, they spoke English without any foreign accent. My brother and sister-in-law never lost their Polish accent. Eventually their English was more than adequate.

My oldest brother, Adam, immigrated to the U.S. in 1986 with his wife, Marysia, and his younger daughter, Magdalena (Magda) who was 16 at the time, the same age as I was upon my arrival to the U.S. Adam's oldest daughter, Joanna (Joasia), was already married in Poland, so she did not join the family in the U.S. until 1990. She and her husband immigrated when Joasia was 27 years old. From observing my family, I conclude that older people have a much harder time adjusting to a new country and learning the language. Also, youngsters who are pre-puberty end up speaking without a foreign accent, while those past puberty never lose all traces of a foreign accent. Adult immigrants seem to have the heaviest accent.

Overall, my brothers' families adjusted well to their new country, and everyone obtained American citizenship as soon as they became eligible. Adults worked and the kids went to school. They all became self-sufficient due to their hard work and pride. No one was looking for handouts, even though their jobs were not particularly lucrative. Stu and I were by far, most economically successful, but my brothers never exhibited any signs of jealousy. They were happy and proud of us. I hosted all the holidays, but they never showed up empty-handed. My sisters-in-law always brought delicious homemade Polish dishes and baked goods.

While they lived in New York, the six of us, Adam, Marysia, Marek, Irena, Stu and I, would arrange dinners out and take turns picking up the restaurant bill. My brothers insisted that they pay the entire bill when it was their turn. Stu and I felt badly, since we knew that they were not as financially privileged; however, we respected the fact that they were proud and not inclined to take advantage of anyone.

Eventually Marek and Irena bought a vacation home in Florida with a plan to retire there. A few years later, Adam and Marysia bought a home in Florida as well. Unfortunately, Marek's health began to deteriorate. He died of a heart attack at the age of 56. It was a family tragedy. My mom was still alive and informing her of her son's death was one of the

hardest things I ever did. He died in Florida unexpectedly.
I wanted to make sure that Mom was not alone when she
heard this horribly painful news, so I invited the whole family
to my house in Manhasset for lunch and went to pick up my
mom in Queens.

Mom was pleased to see the whole family together,
but she must have noticed that everyone was in a somber
mood, despite trying to act normal. She asked, "What's
the occasion?"

I slipped her a Xanax, along with her usual medication
taken at lunchtime. She was sharp and asked why there was
an extra pill. I lied, saying that her doctor told me that this
new medication should be added at lunchtime. When we
noticed that she was feeling the effects of Xanax, I told her
that we had some terrible news.

She asked, "Is it about Marek?" I nodded. "How bad?"

"The worst."

Mom understood. She didn't cry. She spoke slowly and
quietly, "I am glad you are all here, but now I need to be
alone. Please take me upstairs." I did as she requested.

When everyone left, I went up to check on her. She was
curled up on the floor sobbing. She always disliked public
display of dramatic behavior and chose to experience her
sorrow in private. She died two years later. Brother Adam
would live another nineteen years.

Adam and Marysia had a peaceful life in Florida in their
retirement and they were both reasonably healthy. Marysia

didn't drive, so Adam drove her and some of their elderly neighbors everywhere, doctor's appointments, hair salon, and shopping. They visited their daughters in New York periodically most often taking a road trip from Florida and back. Stu and I were always happy to see them either in our home or Magda's. Magda, brilliant nurse extraordinaire, and her husband, Andrzej, have been gracious hosts in their Long Island home, always showcasing Polish hospitality with an abundance of beautifully presented food and plenty of adult beverages cheerfully wrapped in a warm disposition.

In 2019, my brother, Adam, always a gentleman, was helping his wife bring groceries from the car to the house. His hands were full, and he slipped on a step and fell backwards, hitting his head on cement. Magda called me with the sad news of my brother's sudden and accidental death. He was 80 years old. I was playing golf with my girl group when I received the call. I didn't know that one can lose consciousness while standing. My friends told me that after the phone call, I kept repeating, "My brother didn't die" over and over. They escorted me to the club, contacted Stu, and waited for my husband to pick me up. When Stu arrived, he saw that I seemed to be distraught and kept telling him that my brother didn't die. Slowly, on the way home, I became aware of what occurred. I realized that I was the only survivor of my childhood family. Eventually that deep sorrow diminishes and is replaced by sweet memories. I still remember the way my brothers walked, the way their voices sounded and how they smiled and laughed. I was lucky to be their little sister. And they taught me lessons that were capstones in my life.

My brother, Adam, and his wife, my dear sister-in-law, Marysia, visited us in La Quinta in 2006. One evening, I told Adam at dinner that I no longer embraced the Catholic faith. He got terribly upset and responded, "You make me feel as though I spent my life living a lie!"

Calmly but firmly, I replied, "I am not suggesting that you should change your beliefs. I am talking about me and what feels genuine to me."

The next morning, I found my brother sipping his coffee in my family room before anyone else was up. I was worried that he would still be angry with me, so I shyly said, "Good morning."

He was quiet for a bit and then he said, "I couldn't sleep much, after what you said last night. You are a gutsy woman! I respect you, my little sister, because I would not have had the courage to take the big step, which you did." That was it! We never had any religious discussion after that morning. What a gift to have two brothers who loved me as a girl and who respected me as a woman. I think of them a lot as we navigate divisive waters, courageous crossings.

I try hard to be tolerant and non-judgmental towards everyone. The key word here is *try*. I don't always succeed. In particular, I fail to be tolerant when it comes to narcissism. In my view, narcissism can be individual as well as collective. We all recognize individuals who are narcissistic. But some of us may not be aware of being part of a collective narcissism.

In order not to offend any specific group, let's consider a factitious ethnic group called the "Goodies". There are numerous ethnic, racial and religious groups whose members embrace the following credence. Now, Goodies feel superior to all other ethnic groups. The only issues that are significant are those concerning the Goodies. Other people's problems are not of interest or concern. If you are a Goody, you must marry a Goody. Goodies have the best food, the only true religion, the most admirable history, the most talented and clever people. Goodies are never wrong and anybody who criticizes a Goody is an instant enemy. That's collective narcissism in my book! I am a Polish American, but I do not espouse collective narcissism. I find collective narcissism as irritating as I do narcissistic individuals. Well, I am not always tolerant. However, I do my best to respect people whose values and understanding of societal justice differ from mine.

One of my biggest influences in life and most certainly, early years of my American life, Aunt Mary lived until the age of 98. She died in Florida where she spent her old age with her son's family. Unfortunately, she had dementia the last few years of her life, so we didn't communicate. I tried to continue my relationship with my cousin, but he did not seem interested...perhaps our differences were too much. Stu and I and our children enjoy traveling the world and experiencing other cultures and cuisines. We are ethical and spiritual people, but we are not religious. My cousin goes to church every day. His family enjoys fishing and hunting and country life in the Panhandle in Florida. My cousin's wife told me that they are not interested in traveling at all. They are very strongly anti-abortion, while I support a woman's right to be in charge of her own body. Sometimes it saddens me that the only cousin I know is not interested in being in touch with me. I texted his wife over a year ago and she didn't respond. I was sad that they did not let me know immediately when Aunt Mary died. My cousin's wife called me a month later. I would have gone to Florida to pay my respects at her funeral. I truly loved this woman and learned a lot from her. She played such a significant role in my life.

I need to say a few things about my resilient niece, Magda, who came to America like me, when she was sixteen. I love hearing about her experience during a different time period, but fundamentally, our feelings were the same. She says, "Our lives are a million little pieces, and every piece—the journey, the cultures, the desire to leave the country. I was sixteen and there isn't much to say when your parents want to leave. There were minor incidents with the government, but my father was worried about my and my sister's future. Since my father always had an American passport and it was easy for him to travel all his life, he either had to make the move or be too old to do it. They decided to start over when I was a sophomore. My sister, six years older, wanted to stay in Poland and get married. They planned a huge wedding, then we took a leap of faith. At the airport, it was so hot and humid. I remember waiting for green cards, signing a million papers. My grandfather sent a huge car with glorious AC to pick us up. The traffic on the expressway coming from JFK, then the bridges and buildings. The skyscrapers were so different than what I was used to. I was in awe

with every changing frame. What is this wonder? You don't
know if you're going to like it, but your eyes love it! I was so
exhausted from the travel, and I remember my cousin trying
to take me around the neighborhood. The first thing I tried
was ice cream at Baskin Robbins. But first, all the flavors
that you could actually taste before you committed to two
scoops of banana royale and rocky road with whip cream
on top! I was eager to buy cool clothes. The reality though
of not understanding the language yet, missing your friends
and dog, let alone knowing who you are and who you will be
in this new territory, is massive. Poland being a communist
country meant that we were limited in education, jobs,
travel, which was a luxury. You couldn't just leave; you could
be denied a passport to go to the West. My father understood
that very well. He sailed the world. He knew through his
travels that it would get harder as we got older. Us coming to
America did not mean that we would ever lose our memories,
our culture and traditions—it meant that we could always
have more and never be limited. My mom never wanted to
go back to Poland, even for events. She was in control taking
the subway, making money, absorbing cultural events. It's
an incredible gift to have the freedom to do what and how
you want to do it. It's priceless. New York City is a special
place. No one judges you for how different you are or what
your dream is. We take the good with the bad. I spent my
first Thanksgiving at Aunt Marysia's house. She introduced
me to the culture, different foods and opportunities. By
knowing her, you knew anything was possible. She was a
guide for all of us. In this changing world, remember where

you came from. You can always pick out different parts of the journey and think about who came before you and what they sacrificed for you. Get to know your past, your path a little more, which makes the future a little bit more interesting. It carries for generations."

I wonder how many immigrants can relate to Magda's words.

We share our knowledge with each other as we are forever learners. We both believe that it's perfectly fine to change your mind or viewpoint based on your life experience or by gaining knowledge, which we seek all the time.

Some people may feel that after you reach a certain age you cannot change. Stu and I feel just the opposite. One should always try to be better and continue to learn. We often hear some of our friends say, "This is the way I conduct myself because of the way I grew up." They may use this phrase as an excuse for being cheap, or not following proper etiquette, or appreciating finer things in life. Stuart and I never use our past as an excuse. We choose who we are, what we like, what we experience and how we continue to evolve.

Dining, hiking, dreaming in California, 2024.

As we were bringing up our children, we tried to instill in them to be lifelong learners. We gave them skills, such as swimming, tennis, golf, skiing and music lessons. We took them to concerts and sport events. We took them on domestic and European trips. I chuckle at Stuie's words because after all, we taught them to express themselves! He says, "On trips, Mom would have a whole curriculum spanning multiple pages: hit the Louvre, dine at *these* restaurants. At the Louvre, my mom was upset with me because I was crying; I didn't understand why we were there looking at painting after painting after standing in line for an hour. Our idea of having a good time was trying to find the science museum, not going to another old church. We connected later as parents ourselves that our parents wanted us to understand history and culture." And finally, we let them be who they choose to be. We were not perfect parents, but the kids turned out to be good, educated, interesting and fun people.

There is always someone else going through something similar. This is human. You can get over it. There is help. Sharing sorrow builds trust. No matter where we come from, we're similar as humans. The feeling of weakness, failure is common. It's okay to share it with other people. What that sharing looks like varies from person to person. I share with close friends, and you see I've laid out my whole story here! Sharing your life story is not for everyone, but I sincerely hope you've been inspired to think about your own dreams.

My home country was taught resilience. Others in my family reached their potential to whatever was available at that time. In Bytom, those whose families were part of the forced migration spoke with a different accent, more educated, slightly more literary. The people who were forced to live there felt superior to the natives. I grew up so proud of being Polish. Those who used to be German were not authentically Polish. Now, with this statement, I'm provoking what that means for me as a Polish American. What your parents and grandparents tell you shapes your self-image. In America, I "made it" by any standards, and I am a proud American, too, but my parents would always say, well, America is a new country, you come from thousands of years of history and culture. These words can be construed as divisive. I don't want to nourish any shade of bigotry. Who am I as a person? I'm a multifaceted woman. I get offended by Polish jokes, and I'll never let someone in my peripheral put down America, the American dream. Why can't I be all these things? Above all, I'm a resilient dreamer.

References

Association for Women in Mathematics.
"On Women in Math." AWM *Journal*.

https://awm-math.org/.

Editors of Encyclopaedia Britannica. "Opole." *Britannica*. Last
updated: September 24, 2024.

https://www.britannica.com/place/Opole.

______. "Jan Tarnowski." *Britannica*.

https://www.britannica.com/biography/Jan-Tarnowski.

Geology.com. "Poland Map and Satellite Image." *Geology.com*.

https://geology.com/world/poland-satellite-image.shtml.

Hofstra University. "Sylvia Silberger." *Faculty Profiles/
Directory*.

https://www.hofstra.edu/faculty-staff/faculty-profile.
html?id=1398.

Howard, Cheryl. "The Unvertical House in Sopot (aka The
Drunken or Crooked House)." *Cherylhoward.com*. October 1,
2023.

https://cherylhoward.com/unvertical-house-sopot/.

Judt, Tony (2005). *Postwar: A History of Europe Since 1945*.
New York, New York: The Penguin Press, pp. 434–35.

Kowalski, Waldemar, Alicja Rose and Jessica Sirotin. "Stanislaw August Poniatowski, the King Who Wanted to Repair the Commonwealth: An Interview with Professor Richard Butterwick." *Polish History.*

https://polishhistory.pl/stanislaw-august-poniatowski-the-king-who-wanted-to-repair-the-commonwealth/.

Lewis, Paul. "The Lure of a Dollar in Poland." *The New York Times.* October 9, 1981, Section D, Page 1.

https://www.nytimes.com/1981/10/09/business/the-lure-of-a-dollar-in-poland.html.

Library of Congress. "The Nation of Polonia." *Library of Congress.*

https://www.loc.gov/classroom-materials/immigration/polish-russian/the-nation-of-polonia/.

Marx, Willem. "Nearly 120 million people were displaced around the world in 2023, UNHCR report says." NPR. June 13, 2024.

https://www.npr.org/2024/06/11/nx-s1-5002273/nearly-120-million-people-were-displaced-around-the-world-in-2023-unhcr-report-says.

Opera Base. "Opera Śląska, Bytom." *Video Files.*

https://www.operabase.com/opera-slaska-o10041/videos/en.

Photomath. "What is Calculus? Definition, Applications, and Concepts." *Photomath.com.*

https://photomath.com/articles/what-is-calculus-definition-applications-and-concepts/#:~:text=In%20simplest%20 terms%2C%20calculus%20is,calculus%20puts%20 movement%20into%20math!.

Polish History. "Union of Krewo (Act of Kreva)." *Polish History.*

https://polishhistory.pl/union-of-krewo-act-of-kreva/.

Polish Tourism Organisation. "Opole." *Polska.*

https://www.poland.travel/en/opole-history-and-song-festivals/.

U.S. Department of State. "Justice for Uncompensated Survivors Today (JUST) Act Report: Poland." U.S. *Department of State.*

https://www.state.gov/reports/just-act-report-to-congress/poland/.

United States Holocaust Memorial Museum. "The Nazi Party." *Holocaust Encyclopedia.*

https://encyclopedia.ushmm.org/content/en/article/the-nazi-party-1.

Weiss, Brian L. *Same Soul, Many Bodies: Discover the Healing Power of Future Lives through Progression Therapy.* New York, New York: Free Press. October 26, 2004.

Weiss, Tarnopolska Marysia. "On the Number of Lattice Points in a Compact Dimensional Polyhedron." *Proceedings of the American Mathematical Society.* Volume 74, Number 1, April 1979.

https://www.ams.org/journals/proc/1979-074-01/S0002-9939-1979-0521885-3/S0002-9939-1979-0521885-3.pdf.

Wikipedia. "Ternopil Castle." *Radianska Ukraina.*

https://en.wikipedia.org/wiki/Ternopil_Castle.

Wilson Center. "Gomułka, Władysław." *Digital Archive.*

https://digitalarchive.wilsoncenter.org/people/gomulka-wladyslaw.

Wrobel, Piotr (2014). *Historical Dictionary of Poland 1945-1996.* Routledge.

www.ingramcontent.com/pod-product-compliance
Lightning Source LLC
Chambersburg PA
CBHW061425160726

47995CB00003B/755